The Nature of Music

Maureen
McCarthy Draper

RIVERHEAD BOOKS
NEW YORK

The Nature of Music

BEAUTY, SOUND,
AND HEALING

RIVERHEAD BOOKS
Published by The Berkley Publishing Group
A division of Penguin Putnam Inc.
375 Hudson Street
New York, New York 10014

A list of credits and permissions can be found on page 228.

Copyright © 2001 by Maureen McCarthy Draper
Book design by Jennifer Ann Daddio
Cover design © 2001 Tom McKeveny
Cover painting: Gustav Klimt, *Die Musik*, 1895, reproduction © Artothek

Published simultaneously in Canada.

First Riverhead hardcover edition: February 2001
First Riverhead trade paperback edition: November 2001
Riverhead trade paperback ISBN: 1-57322-898-2

Visit our website at www.penguinputnam.com

The Library of Congress has catalogued the Riverhead hardcover edition as follows:

Draper, Maureen McCarthy.
The nature of music : beauty, sound, and healing /
Maureen McCarthy Draper.
p.   cm.
ISBN 1-57322-170-8
1. Music, Influence of.   2. Music—Psychological aspects.
3. Music—Philosophy and aesthetics.   I. Title.
ML3920.D81   2000   00-056036
781'.1—dc21

PRINTED IN THE UNITED STATES OF AMERICA

10   9   8   7   6   5   4   3   2   1

Acknowledgments

Gratitude first to my agent, Katherine Boyle, whose query, "Have you thought about writing a book?" planted the seed. She kept the vision and provided warmth, wit, and good judgment throughout the long writing process.

Love and gratitude to my great-hearted husband, Paul, who read countless versions and somehow remained enthusiastic. He and our daughter Caitlin provided the love and showed saintly patience waiting for dinner.

Having Wendy Carlton as my editor at Riverhead Books was a stroke of good fortune. Her skill and diligence brought focus and polish to the book. To you, Wendy, my sincere gratitude. Thanks, too, to your conscientious assistant, Venetia van Kuffeler.

I'm deeply appreciative of my teachers: Ruth Hardy Funk, the first and most important; Bernhard Abramowitsch; Paul Hersh; Julian White; and Hans Boepple. Associating with such people is reason enough for studying music. And to my students, thank you for making sure that I teach what I need to learn.

I've been supported by many friends, some who have

read the manuscript and made valuable comments: Ted Andersson, Nora Cain, Suzanne Doyle, Anita and Sol Feferman, Kenneth Fields, Nancy Flowers, Rosemary Hayes, Helen Handley Houghton, Susan McDonald, Clare Morris, Elli Norris, Nils Peterson, Constance Pratt, Susan Renfrew, Judy Staples, Kate Strasburg, and Josephine and Denny Zeitlin. A special thanks is due David Lawrence, who was not only generous in sharing his deep understanding of music but cheered and amused me when my energy flagged. To those I haven't named, who, over glasses of wine and cups of coffee, confided what music has meant to them, thank you.

Praise be to Sorensen's Resort, in Hope Valley, California, for the cabin, beautiful scenery, and good vibes.

Thomas Moore is the spiritual godfather of this book. I'm indebted to his understanding of the work of art as a garden or sanctuary. In *The Planets Within, Care of the Soul*, and other books in which he unites soul and spirit, he points the way to living more fully our extraordinary everyday lives.

Contents

. . . and I would give you the gift of music that you might know your own soul

BETH KINGSLEY HAWKINS

Introduction

There is another world and it is within this one.

PAUL ELUARD

I have searched for meaning everywhere. Life has insisted on it. But in the thrall of a great musical moment it has never occurred to me to ask if it has meaning. An experience that brings a heightened awareness of the vibrance, beauty, and wonder of life is always meaningful—an end in itself. Troubling inner voices grow silent when music gives expression to inarticulate thoughts and feelings. Moments become ordered and connected. Existence is felt more keenly.

My first memory of music that made my heart beat faster was hearing what I now know to be Rossini's *William Tell Overture* as the Lone Ranger and Silver made their mad gallop to the top of the bluff every week. Heigh-o Silver! Now it's more likely to be a Beethoven or Mahler symphony that gives me such elation. This book explores the ways in which stimulating music acts on us, viscerally and psychologically—why it can lift a dark mood or give rest to an anxious mind.

Emotions are more manageable when music gives them an objective reality outside us. A seventeenth-century Spanish king had to hear a celebrated tenor, Farinelli, sing every day before he considered himself fit to meet his court. Are we so different, when a few minutes of Bach, Mozart, or Beethoven can bring us back into balance and reestablish our sense of the essential goodness of life? We may not understand what comes over us, why our body relaxes or why our heart melts at the sound of a certain melody or chord change. But when music puts us in harmony with our deepest nature we feel more authentic, more fluid and responsive.

Although music can bless us every day, we hear more and more about its healing power at times of special need—during grief, loss, and illness. A new field, psychoacoustics, is studying the effects of sound on consciousness, and the medical world is using music to reduce stress and anxiety, increase immune-system response, and lower blood pressure and heart rate. Music is helping to counter the trauma of surgery, chemicals, and radiation therapy, and to energize healing techniques using guided imagery. We're also learning about the success of sound therapies—from using singing bowls to freeing our own voices for self-expression. And in this book, I suggest that we expand our notion of the healing power of music to include the pleasure it gives— whether that means being calmed, challenged, stimulated, or transported. The heightened sensitivity music can create, beyond what we ordinarily experience, is itself healing, stimulating our deep reserves of energy.

I will explore many approaches to music, and each of you will respond to different ones. Some ask that you listen to music in ways that may be new to you; others ask for your willingness to use your voice and body to experiment. Focus on those that awaken the music in you, but try to be open to all of them. The more you listen, the more you will hear. Great music continues to unfold in time.

Every day holds intimations of paradise—the scent of a rose, the colors of a sunset, the sound of music—but can we find meaning in these glimpses of glory amid the chaos of tragic events? Can music really help us cope with whatever life brings? And is there music of such ineffable beauty that it can counter and transform fear and suffering? If, as Joseph Campbell says, "the first function of art is to transport the mind past the guardians—desire and fear—of the paradisal gate,"[1] we must seek expressions of love powerful enough to stand up to the cherubim barring entry to the garden. This book is about music that can transport us and how we can benefit from its power.

Without always knowing why, we seek beauty in various forms all our lives. Our hunger sends us to concerts and record stores, to museums and gardens, to faraway places and unlikely teachers, in search of whatever we think will improve the quality of life. Too often we are disappointed. But we must take our longing seriously: it may be as biological as our need for light. Emerson called beauty the "pilot of the soul"—it's the force that drives us not only to music, art, and poetry but to our most rewarding relationships. It even determines the ways in which we spend our time and money. Certainly beauty is one way the divine reveals itself to us. The religions of the world have long recognized the value of stained glass, art, and music as a source of inspiration to worship. Music itself has a religious dimension, satisfying a longing for something that points beyond the temporal to the eternal.

Composers know how to use harmony and melody like a net to catch beauty's colors and radiance. And when we like what we hear, we open our pores to take in more—just as we close them against what seems ugly or offensive. Isn't that why we remember so vividly the hours or days spent in places we love, perhaps in the mountains or by the sea, where all our senses were awake? Where is beauty located? Everywhere we recognize it: the pattern is in us. Beauty is the name we give our response to the perfection we sense around us, and within us. No one embraced this idea more passionately, more eloquently, than Saint Augustine:

> I have learnt to love you late, Beauty, at once so ancient and so new! I have learnt to love you late! You were within me, and I was in the world outside myself . . . You were with me, but I was not with you . . . You shed your fragrance about me; I drew

breath and now I gasp for your sweet odour. I tasted you, and now I hunger and thirst for you. You touched me, and I am inflamed with love of your peace.[2]

At times we may fear beauty. It asks so much of us. In his poem about a stunning bust of Apollo, Rainer Maria Rilke says the demand of beauty is nothing less than that "we must change our lives." Yet we all struggle with the fear of change. Beethoven not only believed his music could transform those who heard it, but that the process of creation would change him as well. The Cavatina* from his String Quartet, Opus 130, reflects the calm of a heart that had learned to listen deeply enough to find a resting place in peace and beauty. A true appreciation of this music can give us more than golden moments. It can give us the courage to bring our highest aspirations into form. And the passion in great music like Beethoven's late quartets reminds us that something beautiful and something eternal wants to be nourished within our hearts.

But what does all this have to do with our daily lives, with the happiness of our children, the well-being of the world? Everything. Without the presence of beauty and joy in our lives we might not value life enough to preserve its quality. Truth clothed in music, words, and images has a greater capacity to move us. "Art creates beauty and that inspires us to love more. That's why we need it," said Edward Abbey. The perfumed perfection of the Abraham Darby rose in the garden or the sweet sounds of Mozart's Violin Sonata in G major, K.216,* drifting in from the stereo are reason enough to honor and protect life. Beautiful music is the promise of happiness, a doorway through which we can enter the fullness of our being. As any great symphony can remind us, we are so much more than the limited territory our ego marks out for itself. And as our awareness expands, our actions become more conscious.

The asterisks (*) in the text indicate that a musical selection is found on one of the two Nature of Music CDs. (To order, see the back of the book.) Having the music by your side as you read not only will save you the trouble of looking for twenty-five different selections, but will enable you to listen and then return to the book. My hope is that the ideas and the music will intermingle with your own response. The Music Breaks at the end of each chapter suggest specific music for listening as well as ways to listen, including some approaches that may be new to you. Try to keep an open mind as you read and listen. You'll know you are listening deeply when you begin to resonate with the spirit *behind* the notes.

My hope is that this book will help you make better-informed choices about what you listen to, how you listen, and why. To know what music makes you happy is to be able to alter your own reality. The spirit and beauty we hear in music are not just a subjective experience but an expression of a larger force that sustains and animates life. The energy behind the notes is of the same magnitude as that which grows the seed, the tree, and the child. We must take responsibility for inspiring our own vision, and we can begin by choosing to hear music that articulates and supports the greatness of human nature. In *I Asked for Wonder* Abraham Joshua Heschel writes:

> *No one will live my life for me, no one will think my thoughts or dream my dreams. In the eyes of the world, I am an average man. But to my heart I am not an average man. To my heart I am of great moment. The challenge I face is how to actualize the quiet eminence of my being.*

ONE

The Heart of Listening

A tree arose. Oh pure uplifted sense!
Orpheus sings! A towering tree was heard!
All was silent. And even in the silence
a new beginning, signs, and change inhered.

RAINER MARIA RILKE, *SONNETS TO ORPHEUS*,

TRANSLATED BY TED ANDERSSON

AND KENNETH FIELDS

W hen you rush to dress for a concert and brave city
traffic to arrive on time, what is it you expect to
happen when the music begins? What kind of experience
do you yearn for?

I want music to take me beyond the limits of my own experience, to connect me with a larger reality. I want to be
filled with sound, to feel music flowing into every cell. I
want the wonder the composer feels toward life, and the
reverence for craft, to rekindle such feelings in me. I want access to a full spectrum of emotions, from exquisite tender-

ness and sorrow to transcendent power and jubilation. Is this too much to ask of music?

To the eyes, music appears as merely black lines and dots on a page. But these marks are energy capsules waiting to be released, launching waves of sound—from the purity of high notes to the full depth of low notes. Our eyes have lids that close, but our ears are unprotected. Sound vibrations go directly to our core, as body-tensing loud sounds can quickly remind us. Should it surprise us then that we have such strong visceral reactions to music? A simple melody or harmony may summon tears and remind us of people and events long forgotten. A great symphony can stir qualities of our humanity that we need and long to feel: exultation, grief, dignity, compassion, playfulness. At times music brings the gift of self-forgetting, inviting us to slip out of our own skin. But paradoxically, because it connects us with our emotions, music often brings more self-awareness. And it's easier to own our emotions when we meet them through music.

Throughout history, music has been an integral part of rites of passage, graduations, weddings, funerals, and healing and religious ceremonies of all kinds. Music has beckoned us to love and war, to worship and mourning. In carrying the emotional undercurrents of these occasions, music joins them to the larger rhythms of life. Composers understand what sounds will evoke a certain mood or response, what rhythms and harmonies will soothe or boost energy. Music has so many faces. We can turn to Bach for the spiritual support of his unswerving faith, to Mozart for perfected grace and beauty, and to Beethoven and Mahler for courage and drama. We look to jazz and popular artists for relaxation and romantic moods. But whether the music is a long symphonic journey or a short blues improvisation, when it gives us what we need, it is a gift.

The Greeks believed that music came from the gods. The myths surrounding its origins arose from the changes that could be observed in listeners. Using the lyre that was Apollo's gift, Orpheus could soothe wild beasts, make the trees dance, and cause the rivers to stand still. The power of his music was great enough that it persuaded the god of the underworld to release his beloved Eurydice. And to this day music leads us to the underworld of feeling. When we are sad or grieving, hearing music that mirrors our sadness can give meaning and dignity to our experience and remind us we are not alone. When we are bursting with high spirits, music can give focus and form to our joy. Out of this understanding, as early as the sixth century B.C.E., Pythagoras, at his school on the Greek island of Samos, recommended certain instruments and modes (scales) to address his students' needs and personalities. Music in the Dorian mode—D to D on the piano—was believed to stabilize and strengthen character, whereas music in the Phrygian mode—E to E—

was potentially unstabilizing. And today we have ways to measure chemical changes in the body stimulated by listening to music. We know, for example, that music we like can trigger the release of endorphins, the feel-good hormones that act as natural opiates.

Encoded in the language of melody, harmony, and rhythm are the patterns of our emotional intelligence, the ancient structures of the limbic system, where emotions reside. You can see the power of this center in your pets' sensitivity to the emotional temperature of your voice, the communication underlying the words. Music is constantly suggesting to us certain states of emotion as it reproduces them in us. And as emotional habits are formed, they eventually become a part of our character. This is what Aristotle referred to when he wrote that "by music a man becomes accustomed to feeling the right emotions."

Music carries our primal longings for connection and fulfillment, raising our expectations to a peak, perhaps many times in the course of a piece. When music excites our hopes for satisfaction, we may feel teased to be led toward a resolution, only to be disappointed by a false cadence that does not satisfy. But the teasing heightens our desire for what may come. As in sexual arousal and satisfaction, the principles of tension and release are experienced physically *and* imaginatively. We can hear this in any of Mozart's or Beethoven's symphonies. Composers are masterful at raising our expectations to a higher pitch, delaying a climax by pulling back again and again, only to take us to new levels of anticipation and promised fulfillment. Music shares with sexuality this capacity to stimulate the mind and body simultaneously.

Music and the Arts

There is a belief that in the beginning all the arts were one, and it is true: music, poetry, and art do illuminate one another and share the ability to unify body, mind, and spirit. Many artists have found inspiration in a sister art—a different language of the soul. In *A Natural History of the Senses*, Diane Ackerman describes how some writers use music to energize their work. She herself has a different piece of music for the "drawer" in her mind where each current writing project resides, thereby cutting down on warm-up time.

Many visual artists have been attracted to, even envious of, the abstract nature of music. This supports Walter Pater's belief that "all art constantly aspires to the condition of music." Raoul Dufy, Paul Klee, and Wassily Kandinsky all confessed to a fascination with music. And to stimulate their own creative process, painters as different in style as Marc Chagall and Jackson Pollock often worked while listening to music. Chagall said that his style changed when he began listening to Mozart. Color, line, rhythm, and texture in the visual arts have musical equivalents in sound. Jagged, even violent lines convey more conflict and force than smooth, flowing ones, in both arts. In Kandinsky's *Improvisations,* which may be viewed as musical compositions on canvas, the lines and juxtaposed colors create patterns of repetition reminiscent of musical rhythm and vibrating sound waves. And he often makes a sequence of shapes or forms, as in his multiple images of figures riding horses—as a composer often repeats a musical idea in sequence (usually three times, in Bach's music). In his book *On the Spiritual in Art,* Kandinsky made quite literal parallels between music and color: black, for example, represented a different kind of silence than white; light blue was the sound of a flute and dark blue a cello. There are similarities too in the way the harmony of tones in the music of Mozart and Schubert creates an impression of grace and balance, as harmonious color tones do in paintings by Poussin, Ingres, and Klee. To echo some of the spikey lines in the music of Prokofiev, Shostakovich, or Stravinsky, we must look at twentieth-century painters, Picasso, de Kooning, and the abstract expressionists. It's notable that so many visual artists have played musical instruments, among them Titian, Tintoretto, Chardin, Braque, Kandinsky, Klee, and Matisse. There are wonderful photographs and paintings of impromptu string quartets composed of painters sitting amid the chaos of easels, canvases, and studio props.

Who can say how many musical compositions have been inspired by art or literature? Pianist-composer Rachmaninoff said, "In my own composition I am greatly helped if I have in mind a book, a beautiful picture, or a poem." The titles of piano works by Liszt relate their imaginative source to Dante, Petrarch, Raphael, and Michelangelo. Claude Debussy drew inspiration from literature. His opera *Pelleas et Melisande* is based on a play by Maurice Maeterlinck and the orchestral *Prelude to the Afternoon of a Faun* was inspired by a poem by Stéphane Mallarmé. Even more of Debussy's works grew from the suggestion of a painting or picture— the prelude "La Puerta del Vino" (The Gate of Wine) prompted by a picture postcard of a famous gate in Granada, Spain, and "Poissons d'Or" (Golden Fish) by a panel he owned of luminous Chinese lacquer. In sound, Debussy imitated the dreamy qualities of light and air in Impressionist paintings. He achieved a hazy vagueness in orchestral pieces like *Nuages* (Clouds) and echoed Impressionist effects such as shimmering light and shadow by placing fragmentary motives and little flashes of different tone colors side by side. Or he rapidly alternated *pianissimo* (very soft) and *fortissimo* (very loud) passages and sparkling *trills* and *arpeggios*. He also exploited the capacity of the piano's damper pedal to blend and blur tones to suggest fog or mist, as in "Brouillards," when the raised hammers allow the strings to continue resonating.

In the prelude "La fille aux cheveux de lin" (The Maiden with the Flaxen Hair*) Debussy uses a primarily *pentatonic* melody to evoke a dreamy, spacious sound, that is, the scale of five notes produced by playing from F-sharp to D-sharp on the black keys only. Many folk songs are pentatonic, like the tune of "Auld Lang Syne." Here, in the widely spaced chords Debussy uses to support the melody, you can listen for the exotic sonorities of Indonesian gamelan instruments, whose gong and bell-like sound Debussy first heard at the Paris Conservatory in 1889. When you listen to his pieces about water (see the Listening Bibliography at the end of the book) with such titles as "Reflects dans l'eau" (Reflections in the Water) and "Jardins sous la pluie" (Gardens in the Rain), it is easy to understand what he was getting at when he said, "Music has this over painting, that it can represent all the variations of color and light in one go."

Music also uses sound to imitate language (word-painting) or to shape a musical phrase so that it suggests the *idea* of an action or scene. Albert Schweitzer thought Johann Sebastian Bach was the greatest painter among composers. Among the hundreds of passages in Bach's work in which sound imitates meaning, two are particularly notable: one in a cantata containing the words, "I shall stand firm," when Bach repeats the same note four times; another in the "Crucifixus" from the B minor Mass, where the melodic lines slope downward, in imitation of a head bowed with sorrow. Handel's oratorios and operas are also bursting with sound-painting, as are those of Haydn, who makes the music of the hills roll and the raindrops dance in *The Creation*. If you were to look at some of this music as it appears on the musical staff, you would discover that it's not necessary to read music to see note patterns tracing pictures of the galloping horses or singing cuckoos in the text.

Descriptive techniques have continued into the twentieth century. Richard Strauss is masterful at using orchestral instruments to evoke sound pictures in *Don Quixote, Till Eulenspiegel,* and other works. Maurice Ravel uses various instruments, each with a different tone color, to suggest the colors of a sunrise in *Daphnis and Chloe.* Of course, some instruments are naturally associated with particular colors: the rich brass of the trumpet and trombone with bold shades of gold, orange, and red; and the lower pitches of the cello and bass with blue, purple, and darker colors. This can be a bit subjective, of course, and at times the inner eye is challenged to see what we hear. In his *Quartet for the End of Time,* French composer Olivier Messaien evokes sound colors he calls "jumbled rainbows" and "blue-orange lava flows." A description of the Apocalypse according to St. John, the *Quartet* quite miraculously creates a mystical, ecstatic reality words can only approximate. To evoke "the impalpable harmonies of the Heavens" Messaien combines gentle cascades of notes on the piano with the distant sound of the violin and cello playing plainsong of Gregorian chant, which has no fixed rhythm or meter. Remarkably, Messaien wrote and first heard this piece performed when interred in a German prisoner-of-war camp during World War II.

In his choral work, *Lux Aeterna* (used in the film *2001: A Space Odyssey*), another contemporary composer, the Hungarian Gyorgy Ligeti, used different means to create complex sonorities that sound astonishingly fresh. Beginning with a single pitch, he gradually adds other pitches above and below it until a dense mix of sound colors is formed. At times so many pitches are present at once that the quality of pitch itself is absent. It's like looking at a white canvas on which the eye can project all colors.

But whatever the music, it's one artist's truth confronting your own, and potentially affirming, deepening, and expanding your understanding of what it is to be alive. The right music at the right time can be a revelation. And because music reaches us on many levels at once, poetic images come closer to the truth of our experience of music than an appeal to rational language. Like speech, classical music is inflected. So when a conductor or performer interprets a piece of music, he or she is deciding what notes to group together, which to give more or less emphasis to, and what dynamic shape to give them in order to make them better understood—just as you do with words when speaking. Although musical language is not denotative, as speech is, it has its own inner logic. If you grew up hearing or singing music, you learned its structures of meaning as naturally as you learned to speak. That's why almost anyone who was raised around Western music knows what the last note of "Happy Birthday" or "Row Row Row Your Boat" should be. Even simple folk songs set up clear expectations that certain notes and harmonies will follow others.

But describing the arrangement of notes or harmonies in a piece doesn't explain the mystery of its effect on us any more than describing grammatical categories such as nouns, verbs, and modifiers elucidates an image in Shakespeare. Good listening is a deeper experience than the ability to stick the correct labels on things. The heart as well as the head must be involved. When a memorable performance of a great piece such as Beethoven's Trio in B-flat, Opus 97 (the Archduke), opens our hearts and minds, it challenges us to transcend the limits we may have imposed on who we are, on what we can embrace. Although every great composer would express it differently, this is the high purpose to which music calls us.

But before we can talk concretely about music, some terms are necessary. You may also consult the glossary in the back of the book for any of the terms in italics.

The Language of Music

The most basic property of musical sound is *pitch*, the highness or lowness of a sound, and an *interval* is simply the distance between two pitches. *Do* to *re* is a small interval, a second; *do* to *sol* is a larger interval, a fifth (*do, re, mi, fa, sol*—five). *Dynamics* refers to the loudness or softness of a pitch. *Rhythm* refers to tempo and pulse, and to the patterns of long and short musical sounds. Rhythm is also the structural force that organizes the phrases and sections of a composition into a form. Like music, we too are rhythmic creatures, and we live in a natural world of rhythmic cycles. From the time our bodies are rhythmically rocked to sleep as infants to the rockings of sexual excitement, from rock concerts to rocking chairs, regular rhythms put us in order. When we respond to musical rhythm it is often below the waist; the legs and feet naturally want to move to what they hear. Composer Roger Sessions argued that movement is as basic to music as sound.

Melody is the horizontal movement of sounds that conveys the narrative of the music. Following a melody from note to note is like following a road. Some melodies arrive at their destination via few bends or curves, while others twist or turn back on themselves, like the loops of Carmen's sinuous "Habanera." When two or more melodic lines move simultaneously, they create a texture called *counterpoint*. Bach is the greatest master of this style, also known as *polyphony*, a reference to its many lines. Because this way of composing can be complex and requires considerable practice, it is known as the *learned style*. Polyphony has been admired and imitated by composers from Mozart and Beethoven to jazz artists such as Keith Jarrett and John Lewis, who recorded jazz improvisations based on the preludes and fugues from Bach's *Well-Tempered Clavier* and *Goldberg Variations*.

An *aria* is a song for soloist and orchestra. In the way it isolates and focuses individual feeling, it became the primary expressive form in the opera. Characters can express their separate feelings and yet blend into a musical whole in a duet, trio, quartet, or even a sextet. The simultaneous combination of tones of different pitches and the successive sounding of these combinations is *harmony*. It can be as simple as singing a third below or above a melody, as we do when harmonizing a camp song or Christmas carol such as "Deck the Halls." When we refer to the harmony of a piece we are talking about its *chords*, vertical combinations of tones played simultaneously. When Schubert drops from a C major to a C minor chord, he only changes one note (lowering the third by a half-step), yet this change can break our hearts. Most often all the elements—rhythm, melody, harmony—are present at once, and at a speed *(tempo)* that can range from very slow to galloping.

Timbre refers to the *tone color* of a voice or instrument, which affects the quality of its sound. Every tone produced by an instrument has a different vibrational pattern, and this gives it a distinctive color. The sound waves a flute produces make smooth, rounded waves on an oscilloscope. A bell or human voice produces more choppy waves that make sharper peaks and valleys. Timbre gives personality and uniqueness to a tone, making the voice of an oboe different from that of Maria Callas.

"Music is the pleasure the human soul experiences from

counting without being aware it is counting," said Leibniz. But it is what music does *with* time that interests us—who are always short of time because we don't know how to stop it. Sometimes life resembles a swiftly moving train that slows or sometimes seems to halt only at moments of intense awareness: joy, pain, or boredom. Composers can control the speed of the train. They can shape a phrase so that it seems to disappear into the distance by marking it with a *ritardando,* to gradually slow down, or a *decrescendo,* to gradually get softer. A composer may delay the resting place of a *cadence,* a stopping point, or expand a moment by using *trills,* two adjacent notes played in quick alternation. The effect of this is to suspend time, as Beethoven does in his last piano sonatas, No. 30, Opus 109, and No. 32, Opus 111. These techniques shape a phrase, giving a string of notes a moving, breathing reality. For the aim of music, whether linked to a religious text or to some other narrative, has always been to stir our feelings in a specific way.

Knowing the period of a composition—Baroque (1600–1750), Classic (1750–1820), or Romantic (1820/ 1830–1900)—makes it easier to predict certain things about its style and structure. These dates are only approximations, but they are a useful rough guide. The relative formality of music in the Baroque and Classic eras reflects the importance given to degree, status, and rules of conduct during those times. By the time of Mozart and Haydn in the Classic period, music had developed a vocabulary of characteristic musical gestures, *topics,* associated with feelings and *affects* similar to the subjects used in rhetoric, including joy, hope, despair, yearning, and fear. The measure of a composer's mastery of craft was in being able to compose music that would evoke any emotion. This is an important point: what Mozart was really feeling when he wrote a sad or happy piece was not supposed to get in the way. And this distinguishes the more autobiographical music that began with late Beethoven and continued into the Romantic period from Classic and Baroque music.

Of all musical genres, dances are perhaps the most popular, perhaps because we like music to move us physically as well as emotionally. Suites of dance music were all the rage during Bach's time, and his suites and partitas brought together dances from all over Europe. In the eighteenth century, Mozart and Haydn were still using dance forms, as well as other musical styles—the *galant,* French overture, German, Italian, *learned,* military, pastoral, Turkish, and church style. To distinguish these styles requires some training, but an ability to hear broad differences requires only a willingness to listen. Certain instruments are associated with particular genres of music, for example, the use of French and English horns to suggest hunting horns and, by extension, the countryside. Mozart would have been aware of these associations in choosing the instruments for his Rondo for Horn and Orchestra, K. 514.*

If you are alert and attentive, you'll pick up differences in style intuitively, the way you appreciate styles of architecture without formal training when you admire a beautiful building for its form and design, for the atmosphere or spirit it creates. You can recognize in a string quartet by Haydn or Mozart, for example, an intelligent conversation between four people with polished, elegant manners; a conversation characterized by the grace, playfulness, and humor of the Classic era. On the other hand, in a quartet by Beethoven the conversation is rife with conflict and differences of opinion, with sudden mood changes and less concern with etiquette. From Beethoven onward, music moved toward greater self-projection. It became more acceptable for an artist to express personal emotions more directly, and sometimes in new forms. Some of Beethoven's late piano sonatas flow organically into one another, without the breaks between movements we've come to expect.

Music is traditional in that it builds on what has come before. If you are a newcomer to classical music you can prepare your ears to hear the patterns in Classic, Romantic, and contemporary music by listening to early eighteenth-century music, such works as Bach's *Brandenburg Concerti*.* Like other compositions from the Baroque period, the musical lines are clearly stated, with repeated patterns and sequences that are easy to pick up. The structure in this music engages the mind, and the Baroque beat and appealing melodies energize the body, making it a natural mood-lifter. Schumann's counterpoint could scarcely exist without the example of Bach, whose music Schumann played every day. And Chopin's piano Preludes, like Bach's keyboard preludes that inspired them, establish and maintain a single mood throughout. Beethoven's ambitious fugues usually come at climactic moments, as at the end of the Piano Sonata No. 31, Opus 110, and the String Quartet, Opus 59, No. 3. It's one way he acknowledges the influence of what he has learned from Bach. A familiarity with Bach and Mozart, who brought together and perfected many musical styles and currents, prepares you to hear what was new (and shocking) in Beethoven and Schumann to ears nursed on Baroque and Classic music. But to say that there was a growing freedom in musical style is not to say that this necessarily led to greater music. We still turn to the music of past masters, as we do to Shakespeare and Rembrandt, for content that doesn't age.

We are fortunate today in having orchestras that can re-create the sounds of Baroque and Classic orchestras, using authentic instruments and performance practices from those eras. Wonderful recordings by orchestras such as the Philharmonia Baroque are available, using instruments that are in some cases quite different from their modern equivalents. Period instruments have more kick and bite; the strings sound more stringy and the reeds more reedy.

Listening to Music, Listening to Yourself

Within its various styles, music reflects the inner and outer movements of our lives—the tensions and releases, the comings and goings, the anticipations and arrivals, the disappointments and fulfillments. Music unfolds in the medium of time, as human character does, and through time reveals itself. As music marks off time into coherent measures, shaping and organizing its rhythms and harmonies, so we structure our days, dividing them into minutes and hours. When we yield to the effects of music, we are participating in the composer's re-creation of the flow of events into a coherent form that otherwise might be heard as unconnected. Sometimes, as in the repeated theme of Schumann's *Arabesque*,* where the melodic line rises, peaks, and subsides, we may be satisfied in our expectations. At other times we may be frustrated, as in Wagner's "Liebesnacht" from *Tristan and Isolde*, which denies erotic fulfillment to the lovers, while it tantalizes listeners with the promise of ecstasy. This music goes right to our nerve endings. A performance of *Tristan* always leaves me feeling slightly drugged. The famous unresolved seventh chord only begins to explain the confusion of sensations—involving love, desire, and death—Wagner evokes in this music. It is a meeting with our own soul, what Marcel Proust describes as "that great black impenetrable night. . . ."

In his essay on Mozart, philosopher Søren Kierkegaard says music is both the most sensual *and* the most spiritual of the arts, sensual by nature, in appealing to the senses, as religious zealots have been quick to point out; and spiritual by tradition, having been used in the service of the Church for centuries. In *Tannhäuser,* Wagner uses both kinds of music to present his hero's conflict: the erotic, exciting music associated with Venusberg, and the hymns of the pilgrims en route to Rome for pardon. On the other hand, Mozart's genius was in combining the physical delight of sensuous harmonies with a chaste purity of line that makes the texture feel uncluttered. Listen for this paradox in his Clarinet Concerto, in the trio from *Così fan tutte,** or the Adagio from the Violin Concerto, No. 3 in G major, K. 216.*

The meaning we find in music comes as we respond to its changing rhythms and harmonies, which, like a magnet can pull images and emotions to the surface. In this sense we could say that listening to music is listening to ourselves. Sometimes the feelings that arise are those we have avoided because they're uncomfortable. There are poignant passages in Mozart's and Schubert's music where beauty and pain seem inseparable. The melodic theme of Schubert's G-flat Impromptu (Opus 90)* has the kind of melting beauty the poet Gerard Manley Hopkins suggests when he asks, *How to keep . . . Back beauty, keep it, beauty, beauty, beauty . . . from* *vanishing away?* When music stimulates a strong emotional response it may be touching places in the heart that need to be acknowledged. Healing often comes in waves, and sometimes old wounds that have only partially healed must be returned to. Music such as the Cavatina* from Beethoven's String Quartet in B-flat (Opus 130) challenges us to become larger, to own more of our pain and sorrow, as well as our tenderness and joy. A heart that has broken may contain more of the world.

There is an Hasidic text that refers to the life process as a gathering up of the soul, which is thought to have been scattered throughout creation. Listening to music may help us recognize and recollect forgotten, lost, or unknown parts of ourselves. This is why at the center of a spiritual *and* a musical life is a deep listening within, what Herman Hesse, in his preface to *Demian*, calls a willingness "to hear the lessons which whisper in the blood." To respond to music as we do, we must already have music in our blood.

The Physical Power of Music

My true life is in the unspoken words of my body.
EZRA POUND, AFTER RÉMY DE GOURMONT

What we call music is sometimes just another element in the surrounding noise. It blares loudly from another car, it follows us around airports, offices, and supermarkets. It is seldom really heard, even when it is worth hearing. And when it is, the speed of our lives is as inimical to listening as it is to other kinds of attending. Just as you must slow down to swirl, smell, and taste a glass of wine or to savor the flavors of food, you need to sit and listen if you're to really take in music. And the greater the art, the more of your attention it demands. Too much outer or inner noise overrides the quiet voices that thrive on slower, more sensuous rhythms and require an attitude of receptivity. For what is communicated in the slower movements of Beethoven, as in the blues of Ray Charles, are authentic experiences of what it is to be alive.

Whatever your listening experience, you take music in through the senses. Hearing is like breathing, but through the ears. Sound flows into and throughout your body like oxygen. You can think of the body, with its nerves and heartstrings, as the lyre upon which your life plays. When music comes into this sensitive instrument it can stimulate the life force on the deepest levels. But you must be ready to receive it. And you must listen with your whole body.

Take a few seconds to notice how you are breathing. As you inhale, try to fill your lower abdomen with air and draw it up through your rib cage and into your lungs. Feel the connection from your abdomen up to your lungs. When you're relaxed and breathing freely, it's easier to take music into your heart. Exhale with a sighing sound and feel the release of tension. Let your shoulders drop. The less armored against feelings, the more responsive you can be. Softening the belly is crucial because it allows natural, full breathing. And to exhale fully is a calming technique as valuable a preparation before listening as before meditating. It is the emotion in the music that you want to respond to, not the distracting emotional ripples of the mind. Teachers of meditation tell us that the mind works best when it is spacious and clear, free to move with each moment. This is also true of listening. Goethe said that he didn't really hear Bach until he heard him in a balanced state.

Like a fine Stradivarius or Guarneri violin or cello, a well-tuned body can be a keen receptor of musical nuance. In a live performance, the physical presence and body language of the musicians communicate the music visually as well as aurally. Because music is grounded in the rhythms of the body as well as in the natural world, Yo-Yo Ma has spoken about how, playing the Bach Unaccompanied Cello Suites, he feels the muscular movements of walking and running, dancing and galloping, rising and falling, as well as the movements of rivers, clouds, and shifting light. Ma's facial expressions as he plays also dramatize these meanings.

In addition to the visual clues we get in a live performance, up to twice as many overtones are audible than in recorded or electronically produced sound. No wonder a live performance can be so much more powerful than a recorded one. *Overtones* are the secondary pitches that also vibrate when a note is sung, struck, or played. When, for example, a low C is played on the piano, the C, G, and E strings above it are among the other strings that vibrate. Overtones are what give warmth and vibrance to a sound, and their absence can make recorded music sound hard and brittle—what struck Stravinsky as "castrated" sound. But a live performance has other attractions. There are risks—a performer's memory may fail or a string may break. As Debussy's irreverent creation, Monsieur Croche the Dilettante Hater, writes, "There is always a hope that something dangerous may happen. . . . Mr. Z may conclude his piece by lifting the piano with his teeth."

Although we know something about how the ear receives incoming sound waves and how the brain interprets them, how the body as a whole reacts is an area of speculation. From the experience of New York Philharmonic percussionist Evelyn Glennie (and others with seriously impaired hearing), we do know that the entire body absorbs and "hears" sound. That's why audial testing measures both bone hearing (which is received through the skull) and air-conducted hearing. Though deaf, Glennie learned to "hear" pitches in different parts of her body, low sounds in the lower body and high sounds in the upper body and head. This should not surprise you if you've been in a concert hall or cathedral where a great organ was being played and you felt the low notes rumbling in the pit of your stomach. In proximity to any vibrating instrument, from a big, operatic voice to a drum or a flute, your body registers sound. I have a resonant frame drum with which I like to give people "sound massages." And if you have ever participated in a drumming circle, you know how thrilling it can be to share the same field of vibration with others.

Sound vibrations can change the structure of a material. You may remember the physics experiment in which you strike a metal plate and watch the ensuing vibrations arrange random sand particles into complex patterns—or the Memorex commercial in which a singer shatters a glass. Such phenomena offer clues to how sound waves may affect our cells. Because sound travels more rapidly through water, and the body is over 70 percent liquid, we humans are excellent sound conductors. Our heads are especially resonant chambers, as you may experience simply by closing your lips and humming. And if you ever get the chance, slip under a grand piano and lie there while it is being played, as I invite people to do in my music retreats. From under a piano the body registers the smallest vibrations in the soundboard, which responds to every change in volume and pitch. If plants and animals respond more favorably to certain sounds than others, as numerous studies indicate they do, it shouldn't surprise us that we do, too. There are healers who use sound to treat various mental and physical disorders, and who knows what the future holds? Someday sound vibrations may be used to stimulate energy in specific areas of the body or to break up tumorous masses.

MUSIC BREAK

Breathing in the Beauty

The heart is the most sensitive ear. Listen to the tender but passionate Brahms Intermezzo, Opus 119, No. 1,* letting your belly soften and your breath flow easily. Feel you are listening with all the pores of your body. Now breathe the music into your heart and let your breath follow the rise and fall of the melodic lines.

TWO

Hearing the Design

Isn't form a talisman against disintegration?

RITA DOVE

Making things, constructing forms, is an innate human tendency. Pots, pictures, and pieces of music are among the ways we fulfill our need to hold back something from the flow of life, for contemplation and appreciation. The inexhaustible richness of life feeds our appetite for discovering the designs and proportional harmonies in the natural world, in art and architecture. We find similarities between the spirals of hurricanes and nebulae, those of a nautilus shell and the center of a daisy, between the branching patterns that segment, divide, and recombine in leaves, trees, and rivers. Musical designs take hints from the natural world, and like organic forms, music may grow from a single seed, each part in relation to the whole. Yet music is a human construct, a more highly organized version of our experience.

The shapes of music—songs, dances, rondos, fugues, and sonatas—have evolved over time, but as a good chef makes imaginative variations on a classic recipe, a skillful composer makes inherited forms his own. A melody may have begun as a popular tune, but when adapted by Schubert, Brahms, or Stravinsky, it's taken to a more complicated level of organization, as with the folk songs Stravinsky uses in *The Wedding*. If there were not an art to thinking in sounds, we could not distinguish greater from lesser compositions. Musical thinking, like other kinds of thought, can be logical or intuitive, congruous or incongruous, inventive or clichéd. The delight we feel in hearing a piece of music depends on the relationship between the sounds and the effectiveness of their expression. Is the emotional palette subtle and complex? Is the music many-sided, presenting different aspects of itself at different moments? If, as T. S. Eliot said, hell is a place where nothing connects, then great music is a paradise of connections and relationships.

Music is sound *and* silence. It is the spaces *between* the notes that create rhythm, melody, and meaning, and the greater the composer—and the performance—the better the quality of the silence. Legendary pianist Artur Schnabel said that it wasn't the notes but the silences between them he played better than other people. A few seconds more or less at crucial moments in the performance of a piece may mean the difference between a mundane and a transcendent experience.

As hours organize minutes, *meter* divides musical time into *measures*, groups of beats marked off on a score by a vertical line. Meter controls and manages time, ordinarily throwing the accent onto the first beat of each measure. When the rhythm is syncopated, the accent is shifted to a weaker beat. Syncopated rhythms carry the flavor of jazz, whether the music is by Stravinsky, Gershwin, or Bernstein. Stravinsky said that his enthusiasm for American jazz influenced his choice of instruments in his popular work, *The Soldier's Tale*, which include a clarinet, trumpet, trombone, and percussion—a version of a jazz band. The slight hesitation in a phrase, the delayed downbeat, or the missing but implied note of a melody in Gershwin's *Rhapsody in Blue* or Bernstein's *West Side Story* are the kind of jazzy effects that get under our skin. Meter creates symmetry, and symmetry is the norm that makes asymmetry possible, the order against which deviations can occur. Aren't our lives composed in similar ways, observing rules but straining away from them for the sake of diversion, creativity, or mischief? Don't you relish a surprise more when you're expecting something predictable to happen?

As the very texture of our lives, contrast is a basic organizing principle in musical form as well. You can hear it everywhere, from the eighteenth-century dance suites Bach composed for cello, violin, and keyboard to contemporary sonatas and symphonies with contrasting movements. Inward, majestic, or lyrical slow movements tend to alternate with faster ones that may be light, rustic, or robust. When you listen to the Allegro* from Bach's Brandenburg Concerto in F major or any of the faster movements from his Unaccompanied Cello Suites, you're able to experience what it's like to move from the slow pace of a *sarabande*—a slow dance of Spanish origins in triple meter, often with an accented second beat—to the springy step of a *gavotte*—a Baroque dance in duple meter. And your reaction to a tempo is a clue as to whether your need is for calming or energizing music. It's worth noting that in Baroque music contrasts occur between, not within, movements as they do in the Classic sonata and symphonic forms developed by Haydn and Mozart, where a movement may have two dramatically contrasting themes. But drama is also generated between contrasting movements. Mozart often follows a melancholy Andante or Adagio movement with a lively Rondo, Allegro, or Presto that urges you to get in step *(Will you, won't you, will you, won't you, won't you join the dance?)*. The ravishingly beautiful slow movement from the Piano Concerto in C major, No. 21, K. 467, is followed by the sprightly Allegro vivace; and the Andante of the Piano Concerto in A major, No. 23, K. 488, is followed by Presto.

Beethoven's music draws vitality from the drama of moving *through* tension to resolution. Victor Borge's remark that hearing a Beethoven symphony is like hearing a peace negotiated between a feuding husband and wife is amusing and it hits the mark. Much New Age music takes the opposite approach and tries to eliminate tension. The difference in effect is like that of being dropped by helicopter on the top of a mountain, versus climbing up on your own two legs: we miss the effort of the journey and with it, the anticipated joy of arrival. The serene bliss of the second movement of the Piano Concerto No. 5 (the Emperor) is all the more numinous because it follows the galvanizing drama between piano and orchestra in the first movement. And the first movement of the Third Symphony *(the Eroica)* is a watershed work that miraculously balances the tension of extremely opposing musical ideas. But reconciling differences in mood, topic, and key was at the very heart of the Classic style. The wonder of a symphony like the *Eroica* is that moments of exquisite tenderness, terrible power, and humor can exist side by side. In the drama of the contrasting themes that differentiate, combine, separate, and recombine again and again, each time with increasing energy, our reward is to hear convergences and complexities that echo those within our own soul, woven into a single musical fabric.

Such contrasts keep us surprised, engaged, and awake. Another source of contrast is texture, which Ravel exploits in his String Quartet in F, with an entire movement of *pizzicato* playing. This means plucking the strings with the fingers instead of bowing them, and it makes the violin sound like an entirely different instrument.

Thematic Seeds

A large work may be generated from a simple melodic phrase. Though Bach had the intellect to manage incredibly complicated networks of parts (listen to any of the fugues in *The Well-Tempered Clavier*), he developed his large structures from small thematic seeds of just a few notes. Similarly, Beethoven often opens a piece with a short melody from which an entire work grows. Music teachers like to illustrate the use of this technique in Beethoven's Fifth Symphony, with its now-famous opening motif of four notes. But we can hear this technique throughout Beethoven's compositions. Three of his late string quartets share a musical motto of four notes that recur in different guises throughout (G-sharp, A, F, E, played by the cello at the opening of Opus 132) and the last three piano sonatas are linked by a motive of falling thirds.

A *fugue* is one of the most highly organized, crafted plans for presenting a theme. Historians have suggested that fugues were so popular in northern Germany during Bach's time because they represented a model of order to a people who had known the chaos and disorder of decades of war. The initial subject (theme) may be a simple enough melodic idea, but the combined parts (voices) can become complex textures. It's easy to hear the way the subject is stated first by one voice and then imitated in succession by the other voices, repeatedly, throughout the Fugue in C major, BWV 953.* As you listen to how the subject is picked up by each voice, you can also hear other motifs woven into the musical texture. Beethoven often used fugues to impose order after highly expressive, sometimes disruptive, passages of personal revelation—or at climactic points, such as at the conclusion of a work, to increase the emotional heat.[1] Brahms concludes his piano work, *Variations and Fugue on a Theme by Handel*, with a fugue. Schumann, Mendelssohn (in Opus 35), César Franck, Verdi (in the "Sanctus" of his Requiem), and Shostakovich all made their fugal bows to Bach.

Hearing a fugue develop is like watching a densely formed cloud unfold and expand. And the continuous sound of a great organ may be the best instrument for projecting the cumulative power of a fugue. As each voice is added, a great cathedral of sound builds in the ear and fills the body. Often, toward the end, there is a musical traffic jam *(stretto)* as the voices are jammed together, entering in close succession—the musical equivalent of steering three or four cars at once! Some of the most moving, emotionally charged choruses are fugues, Handel's "For Unto Us a Child Is Born" from *The Messiah* and sections of Beethoven's Ode to Joy in the Ninth Symphony.

Circular Forms

The urge to leave home, explore, and return—the circular form of Homer's *The Odyssey*—is a basic pattern of human behavior mirrored in music, as in literature. Beginnings and endings help us organize our lives, and the order of form offers the possibility of rest. A simple example of departure and return is the little song "Twinkle Twinkle Little Star," which begins and ends with the same melody (A). The structure (ABA) shapes countless popular songs, dances, and pieces: the waltzes of Schubert and Chopin and many pieces in Schumann's *Album for the Young*.

The *rondo,* one of the oldest musical shapes, returns again and again to the same theme after intervals of new material (ABACADA, etc.). A poem or song with the same refrain after each new verse is in rondo form. A rondo is like a series of short excursions, with a return home after each one. Listening to Schumann's *Arabesque,* you can hear how the repeated theme of this rondo accumulates nuances of meaning after each intervening section. Every return to the lyrical theme, whose notes are unchanged, is reassuring. It may suggest to you that despite excursions into contrasting moods and character, some constancy or unity persists.

A work of three or more movements in alternating slow-fast tempo may be called a *sonata*. But *sonata form,* the most important form of the Classic era, refers to works in which each key area has distinctive themes. Most first movements of sonatas, symphonies, concertos, and string quartets are in sonata form. In the first section, the *exposition,* the musical themes are introduced in the home key. In the middle section, the *development,* themes are taken through different keys, moods, and situations. Finally, in the *recapitulation,* the themes are repeated in the original key, restoring normality. Sometimes there is also an initial introduction and an extended ending, or *coda.* One movement may be a *minuet*—a graceful dance of French origin in triple meter—as it is in many works by Haydn, Mozart, and Beethoven. But beginning with Beethoven, the minuet was often supplanted by the *scherzo* (the Italian word for "jest"), a lively playful movement.

Although we recognize a snowflake or a leaf by its basic form, we know that no two snowflakes or leaves are exactly the same. Each is a variation of a basic pattern. *Repetition and variation* of a musical theme work in a similar way, and may be the most commonly used form. It is easy to hear a variation on a theme in a hymn, folk song, or dance; more difficult to hear it in a complicated jazz or classical piece. Playing on the idea of identity preserved throughout change, the pleasure we take in the different textures and moods in a set of variations comes from appreciating the composer's skill and invention within self-imposed limits. When part of the melody or harmony is missing, as it often is in a jazz variation, it's assumed that the ear will understand and fill in what's implied. Some of the greatest works are in this form:

Bach's *Goldberg Variations*, Beethoven's *33 Variations on a Waltz by Diabelli*, and Brahms's *Variations and Fugue on a Theme by Handel*. Anchored in the simple reality of a theme, a set of variations allows the composer's imagination to cover a vast emotional territory.

As your outward manner and persona can change in the presence of different people and situations, so a musical theme changes according to its surroundings, sometimes even beyond recognition. Among the ways a composer can alter musical texture are by changing the mode (major or minor), tempo (fast or slow), register (high or low), harmony, and meter (3/4 or 4/4, etc.). Beethoven often uses only part of the theme *(fragmentation)*. In almost all sets of variations the theme is stated at least once in a minor key, giving it a darker sound. A busy, florid texture can be achieved by using notes of shorter duration *(diminution)*. But even when repetition exists physically, it is never quite the same psychologically. What happens to the original theme along the way changes the way it is heard. When Bach concludes the *Goldberg Variations* with the same aria with which it began, the aria has been illuminated by all the colors, nuances, and permutations of rhythm and harmony of the preceding thirty variations. It is richer, broader, and more numinous.

I have witnessed performances of the *Goldberg Variations* that affect audiences like a religious experience. The music creates a sense of presence that connects listeners with transcendental energies. Martin Luther said that theology begins at the place where music takes us. Gifted, eccentric Polish harpsichordist Wanda Landowska, whose celebrated interpretations of the *Goldbergs* inspired a cultlike following, used to wear a special red velvet gown and red shoes to honor each performance. Glenn Gould, another gifted musician whose playing of Bach made him a legend in his lifetime, recorded the *Goldbergs* twice, once early and again later in his career because his sense of this music changed as he changed; and each recording has its advocates. But whatever artist you listen to, don't miss hearing this work in its entirety. I think you will discover that each variation whets your appetite for the next—not because it is unsatisfying but because it is so appealing. From a few sounds, Bach creates many worlds.

The Enduring Power of the Mass

What most of us need, almost more than anything, is the courage and humility really to ask for help, from the depths of our hearts . . . to ask for the power to understand the meaning of our suffering and transform it. . . .

SOGYAL RINPOCHE, *THE TIBETAN BOOK OF LIVING AND DYING*[2]

Another form of journey, and one of the oldest, is the Catholic mass. The sections of a mass follow a progress of

the soul from alienation to atonement, a psychological journey of healing that is a perennial need. A mass begins with
the supplicant's request for mercy and forgiveness in the
Kyrie, continues with the confession of belief in the *Gloria*
and the *Credo,* and culminates in blessing and forgiveness in
the *Sanctus, Benedictus,* and *Agnus Dei.* Though it evolved
hundreds of years ago, the mass continues to offer comfort
and bring renewal. Crucial to the healing process, and before
comfort can come, is the petitioner's expressed need for help.
The *Kyrie (Lord, have mercy on us)* is a cry from the soul; we
must empty in order to be filled.

The mass expresses a wide range of emotions. This is
one secret of its endurance. Even in the requiem masses,
whose subject is death, a mass seeks a positive approach. For
if art ceases to affirm life, where are we to go? It is evidence
of the appeal and power of the mass that some of the most
beloved have been composed by non-Catholics, Bach and
Beethoven. Among the greatest masses are the B minor Mass
and the Passions by Bach, especially his *St. Matthew,* performed at Easter all over the world; the last six masses by
Haydn; the *Missa Solemnis* by Beethoven; Schubert's Masses
in E-flat and in A-flat; and the requiem masses by Mozart,
Brahms, and Fauré. These works continue to engage us because they address our need for solace, forgiveness, and affirmation, especially at times of loss.

Using music as a vehicle for transcendence, we can create rituals that make our homes true sanctuaries for our souls.

For years at my house it has been a Sunday-morning ritual for whoever wakes first to put on music, usually early music (for a year, it was Monteverdi), a mass, or anything by Bach. We try to stay in silence until noon. It's a time we've come to cherish, an opportunity to pause, reflect, and recollect our scattered selves.

Yesterday's Dissonance Is Today's Consonance

Masses, symphonies, and sonatas still have vitality for composers as well as listeners—though a symphony by a contemporary composer such as Lou Harrison may use the gong and bell-like instruments of the Indonesian gamelan orchestra rather than traditional instruments. Composers through the ages have stretched existing forms and created new ones. And for this they have often been berated.

As inevitable and aesthetically beautiful in proportion and expression as Beethoven's music may seem to us now, his compositions were described by some of his contemporaries as "barbarous," "bizarre," "incoherent," "shrill," "chaotic," and even "ear-splitting." I quote from Nicolas Slominsky's *Lexicon of Musical Invective,* a historical primer of insults, many from accounts of first performances of what are now mainstream classical works. Beethoven's late piano sonatas (Opus 109, Opus 110, and Opus 111) were shockingly personal by the standards of the Classic era, and they were first heard by a nineteenth-century Viennese audience who, for the most part, did not consider them to be serious music. With successive hearings we often come to feel more positively about a work, but in the opinion of composer Gioacchino Rossini, whose own operas were unquestionably shorter and easier to digest than Wagner's, "One can't judge Wagner's opera after a first hearing, and I certainly don't intend going a second time."

Sometimes a new work is judged to have too much *dissonance,* a word used popularly to refer to harmonies we don't like, or to sounds that seem offensive. In his autobiography *Memories, Dreams, Reflections,* Jung recorded his reaction to the dissonance in a concert he attended:

> *I sat and listened, fascinated. For far more than an hour I listened to the concert . . . soft music, containing, as well, all the discords of nature. And that was right, for nature is not only harmonious; she is also dreadfully contradictory and chaotic.*

Musically, *dissonance* refers to intervals or chords that create tension because they are unstable and therefore generate the energy to move—the opposite of *consonance,* in which sounds are relatively stable and free of tension. To be sure, more dissonance has entered classical music since 1750, as music has included more of the sounds of modern life.

Yet one person's dissonance may be another's ecstasy. Arnold Schoenberg's music is championed by many musicians, and his early works such as *Transfigured Night* have lush, late-Romantic harmonies that please most audiences. Fewer find pleasure in his later, *atonal* works, which lack the tonal center that has organized music for centuries. But the wider our listening experience, the more tolerant of tonal complexities and discord we may become. Like some modern visual art, contemporary music is not always pleasing, but it may be adding something new to our discourse with the world around us. It's a matter of degree. A piece that has just a few dissonant details, some biting chords or harmonies, can put us pleasantly on edge, but a piece we can't make sense of, in which resolution can't be anticipated, can leave us cold. Some people derive intellectual pleasure from the way atonal works are constructed, but I confess I'm not one of them. Nevertheless, I'll keep listening.

Dissonance is a part of life. Things don't always fall harmoniously into place and you don't always get what you want, when you want it. It is no different for composers, and Mozart is not the only composer to balance moments of perfect beauty and harmony with passages that reflect life's disharmony. I'm thinking of the disturbing melancholy of the slow movement of his Piano Sonata in C major, K. 330, which follows the playful, upbeat first movement. In a crucial cadence before the repetition of the theme he changes only one note in a chord, but that change stabs the heart.

Immediately after this, the piece returns to the cheerful F major theme, as if to say, "But life is too precious for pessimism." But Mozart's use of dissonance is hardly comparable to that in some twentieth-century works that continuously assault our ears. We can argue too that since some dissonance *is* an unavoidable part of our life experience, it makes harmony in music all the more desirable. At the end of a difficult day, most of us long to be soothed, not jangled.

Still, there are times when a touch of dissonance in a melodic line may be excruciatingly beautiful. Certainly Renaissance choral masters such as Thomas Tallis knew this. An interesting example is the use of the tritone, which was forbidden by the Church in early music as "the devil in music" because of the tension it creates. It occupies an uncomfortable place between a fourth (C to F) and a fifth (C to G), and before 1900, was very rarely used in a melody. Leonard Bernstein exploits the tension in this interval to a poignant end in "Maria" from *West Side Story*, using the interval between the first and second syllables of Maria's name. In another moment of beautiful dissonance, Giuseppe Verdi underscores the tragedy of Aida's final aria, "O terra, addio," with the stretched tension of the interval of a seventh. Only a half-step shy of the octave, a seventh has the effect of reaching but not quite attaining the peace of consonance. It can suggest anguish, longing, and any number of other emotions at once.

It helps put things into perspective to realize that in his time even Bach was accused of too much *chromaticism*, that is, creating dissonance by using notes outside the key in which a piece is written. Also, realize that Mozart's father and teacher, Leopold, after seeing new compositions by his son, protested Mozart's use of "harmonic progressions, which the majority of people cannot fathom" (in a letter of 1778). The difference between then and now is that Bach and Mozart used dissonance rarely, and only as an expressive device, and the music of the last eighty years is rarely without it. And now dissonance is sometimes left unresolved, which accounts for much contemporary music being gut-wrenching rather than gut-moving. The period between the two world wars was a tumultuous time for music—French composer Henri Dutilleux referred to the "aesthetic terror" of the post-war decades. He meant the way many composers with a strong academic orientation scorned tonality, writing music to fit intellectual concepts, often appreciated only by their teachers. What would Bach, Mozart, and Beethoven have made of the disturbing music by twentieth-century Eastern European and Soviet composers such as Shostakovich, Prokofiev, Schnittke, and Kancheli, which respond to events that include the Holocaust and two world wars?

Because our ears have been taught to anticipate at least a consonant resolution in a work, it's not difficult to construct dissonant chords that produce great discomfort, especially when the clashing tones come at a high volume. The Geneva Convention proscribed the use of intensely loud sounds as a form of torture, and few people will choose to listen to music that causes a high level of unease. What, then, is the place of fear and paranoia in the concert hall? There *are* occasions when we want music to confound our expectations or we look for music to open our minds to new possibilities. But unless we are intentionally trying to break up old patterns of listening or thinking—for which dissonance can be helpful—why should we knowingly choose to hear music that makes us more anxious?

I like to imagine what Mozart's mirthful disbelief would be in hearing compositions by the American Charles Ives. An experimenter, Ives led the way toward a uniquely American sound for twentieth-century composers who were looking for models other than dead Europeans. He pulled out all the stops; for instance, pitting marching bands, each one playing different tunes and rhythms, against one another. Reflecting his creed, "Music is life," Ives tried to pack as much life into a single chord as it could bear, giving us the dubious thrill of amazingly dense sound textures—layers of sound that mingle Baptist hymns, popular songs, marching bands—all the music he might have heard on a Sunday afternoon in the New England town in which he grew up. Mozart would have been in complete agreement with Ives's belief that, as part of a human community, we owe our neighbors all the truth and beauty of which we're capable. But wherever Mozart's imagination and human sympathies took him—and to him we must credit some of the most vivid and dramatic music ever created—he seemed almost incapable of making music that wasn't beautiful. In fact, according to his definition of music, beauty was a requirement. He expressed this aesthetic, a kind of eighteenth-century golden mean, in a letter to his father, dated 1791:

> [P]assions, whether violent or not, must never be expressed in such a way as to excite disgust, as music, even in the most terrible situations, must never offend the ear, but must please the hearer, or in other words, must never cease to be music.

Many of us have come to tolerate, even find pleasure in, a range of sounds, styles, and forms that would have made Mozart cringe. Electronic synthesizers can generate sounds of any kind, some music, some just the noises of life, and this has given composers an immense vocabulary of new sounds: such things as free improvisation by orchestra members, the sounds of gunshots, environmental sounds, cellists rapping on their instruments like drums, pianists noodling mysteriously inside the piano, and singers whose voices have been electronically amplified and distorted beyond recognition. Shostakovich's String Quartet No. 8 bears a dedication "to the victims of fascism and war," and as we might expect, it includes sounds that are as bleak, shrill, and harsh as the events to which they respond. It could be argued that without the tortured circumstances of Shostakovich's life—he never knew when he or his family might be arrested by Stalin for composing music that didn't comply with Communist dictates for art—his music would not have aspired to such tragic heights. You must decide for yourself if his music wrests redemption from bitterness and suffering. Certainly, some passages, like the Andante from his Piano Concerto No. 2, which has been used by dance choreographers, achieve a beauty that is redemptive.

The present Babel of musical styles promises to continue well into the twenty-first century and much that is contemporary may be temporary. But tonality is again one option among others for contemporary composers. There is also a realization that if there are to be audiences for music, their taste must be considered and educated. Historically, the artist's role is to extend a culture's idea of what is true and beautiful. In the 1950s and 1960s, just as many listeners were no longer listening to new music because it seemed arid and academic, seeking relief with Mostly Mozart and early music, a new generation came along that included eclectics, neo-Romantics, minimalists, and tonalists. Audiences were drawn to music they felt they understood, works by Terry Riley, John Adams, Steve Reich, and Philip Glass—in a style known as *minimalism,* which uses many repetitions of simple melodic fragments. Among other well-received contemporary composers today are, in America, John Corigliano, Richard Danielpour, John Harbison, Alan Jay Kernis, and Tobias Picker; in Eastern Europe, Henryk Gorecki, Gyorgy Ligeti, and Arvo Part; in Russia, Sofia Gubaidulina; and in England, John Tavener.

Although this chapter has been about the forms of music, I want to emphasize that to be moved by music is more important than to be able to recognize a sonata or fugue. True listening involves the ear of our heart, not just our mind, and our capacity to respond to Mozart as we do is proof enough that the human heart hasn't changed over the centuries. If we are to continue to turn to music for its spiritual value as well as for pleasure, it must satisfy our human need for beauty, vitality, and affirmation. It must call forth a harmony within us, and among us, that may be deeply buried but is longing to be realized. Above all, music must come from the heart of its creator. The most clever cerebral music may be interesting but is seldom great. It is worth noting that three generations of nontonalists, beginning with Schoenberg, have been unable to counter a habit of hearing that correlates harmony of the spirit with harmony of sound.

MUSIC BREAKS

Fugue or Fudge Ripple

Listen to the lively Little Fugue in C*, imagining the subject as it ripples through the texture of the music like a vein of chocolate in vanilla ice cream.

Returning to the Theme

Listen to Schubert's Impromptu in G-flat, Opus 90, No. 3* and jot down some adjectives about how the opening theme makes you feel the first time you hear it. Use only a few words—relaxed, dreamy, yearning, serene, blissful. Then write a few more words about your mood after the episodes that follow. Finally, what is your feeling when the theme returns?

Experiencing the Power of the Mass

⁓

Take a Sunday morning to experience the full psychological journey of one of the great masses referred to in this chapter. During the cry for mercy in the Kyrie, write a few words about what your own need is, at this moment. And don't hesitate to draw or to dance what you feel at different stages of the mass.

In Your Own Words

⁓

Listen to Brahms's *A German Requiem,* composed at the time of his mother's death. He chose his own biblical texts, those that had special meaning and comfort for him. What healing words from your favorite texts would you choose for comfort if you were writing your own mass?

_____

_____

THREE

The Education of Feeling

Observe, if you please, the order of the development here . . .
it is feeling that sets a man thinking, and not thought
that sets him feeling. . . . All education, as distinct from
technical instruction, must be education of the feeling,
and such education must consist in the appeal
of actual experiences to the senses.[1]

GEORGE BERNARD SHAW

Numerous studies have shown that, as Shaw believed, we learn best when thinking is linked to feeling. And music may evoke our most tender feelings. The subtle emotions, as opposed to fear and anger, came with the evolution of the cerebral cortex, and they express the quality of our humanity. Evolution has created and preserved emotional intelligence as a reliable source of knowledge, and as Daniel Goleman argues in the book *Healing Emotions,* we should value the information it gives us. Music is a way to that source. If music itself doesn't teach us about the depths of the soul, how is it that young musical prodigies can project to an audience emotional complexities they have experienced only through the medium of music? Art doesn't just imitate life; it anticipates it. "Great music," writes musicologist Victor Zuckerkandl, "is written to realize as yet unrealized inner experiences, not to express those already realized."

Music is like a stage on which the basic patterns or archetypal models that underlie the human experience are played out. These are the larger stories we are living, or struggling to live, such as that of the questing hero, like Odysseus, who ventures far from home to fulfill his destiny. Or the archetype of the divine child, the aspect of the soul that knows what it means to be whole and happy. One quality that makes great music so timeless is its uncanny capacity to suggest these universal narrative patterns of exploration and discovery, loss and triumph. Mozart's music often translates heroic effort and strife into intense, thick musical textures, as in the dramatic first movement of the A minor Piano Sonata, K. 310. But the peace and joy associated with the eternal child are communicated in clear, simple textures such as the much-loved slow movement from the Piano Concerto in C, K. 467 *(Elvira Madigan)* or the Adagio* from the Violin Concerto No. 3, K. 216. Tender expression requires a slow and gentle pace.

Dynamic patterns are built into the form of classical symphonies and sonatas. With hierarchical scales and harmonies that move away from and then back to the tonic, or home key, the *sonata form* is always seeking the repose of a final *cadence*. When, after the characteristically heroic struggle of the first movement of his Piano Concerto No. 5 (the Emperor), Beethoven achieves a sublime rest in the second movement, it suggests his victory and, by extension, yours. Changes in harmony, like changes in rhythm and tempo, may affect you profoundly. And you don't have to be able to name a key shift to be moved by it. Indeed, some music is an emotional odyssey that can leave you exhausted or, at other times, exhilarated. If life moves between the poles of love and fear, music should reflect these fluctuations—and it does. In his compelling biography of Mozart, Maynard Solomon speaks of his compositions as having "opposed affects, of beauty and sadness, of consolation and terror, of longing and anger, of pleasure and pain." This description fits many great compositions in the Classic style. And when you respond emotionally to music you are picking up these projections. In "The Concert," Edna St. Vincent Millay tells her lover what she will experience at a musical performance if he doesn't go with her:

> *If I go alone,*
> *Quiet and suavely clothed,*
> *My body will die in its chair,*
> *And over my head a flame,*
> *A mind that is twice my own,*
> *Will mark with icy mirth*

The wise advance and retreat
Of armies without a country,
Storming a nameless gate,
Hurling terrible javelins down
From the shouting walls of a singing town
Where no women wait! . . .
I will come back to you, I swear I will;
And you will know me still.
I shall be only a little taller
Than when I went.

Granted, this speaker was a particularly sensitive listener and a poet. Yet, if you are receptive to music you know how powerful a musical experience can be, sometimes more powerful than one acted out. Even if your listening experience doesn't echo that of a Hollywood epic, as Millay's does, you flesh out what you hear with the stuff of your own soul. And you are limited only by the scope of your imagination. The more richly furnished it is with interior landscapes, characters, and creatures, plots and dramas, the more you experience in music, as in life. And the drama is not confined to the mind; your entire biochemistry can be affected, producing changes in breath rate, blood pressure, and galvanic skin response.

San Francisco Symphony conductor Michael Tilson Thomas has described music as a "psychological landscape." The reasons you gravitate toward certain pieces and not others offer clues to your psyche. In the same way you may be drawn to the mountains, seacoast, or desert because they make you feel more alive, more truly yourself, certain melodies and harmonies may attract you. Some sounds may open up secret inner rooms and gardens. A recent composition by Tobias Picker, *Old and Lost Rivers,* creates such an imaginative space for me. The haunting ambiguity of its harmonies stirs childhood memories of days spent exploring riverbeds in the foothills of the Rocky Mountains. For you it will touch other memories. Music that brings together inner and outer, past and present, helps us feel more integrated, more abundant, and whole.

Arvo Pärt's *Fratres* has a powerful psychological effect of a different kind. In contrast to the relaxed flow of Picker's composition, *Fratres* consists of repeated musical patterns that conjure an intense, ritualistic atmosphere, not unlike that of Ravel's *Bolero.* Pärt's music is introspective, mystical. Works such as *Fratres* and *Cantus for Benjamin Britten* can cast a spell on listeners. After all, virtual realities are not just a recent triumph of cyberspace and Imax theaters. Before now, alternate realities have been designated by such names as *fiction, art, dance,* and *music.* Whether you are drawn into Pärt's absorbing audial space, or you choose to follow Mozart down the path of a ravishingly beautiful melody like the Adagio* from the Violin Concerto, No. 3 in G major, K. 216, music draws you into an imaginative reality. And to the degree that a work can fix experience in a form that moves again *in you*, it succeeds.

Even when music is joined to a text, you may prefer to ignore it in favor of your own inner narrative. Music has the power to stir your emotions, but it is your imagination that organizes the emotions into a story. The warmth and passion in a Brahms Intermezzo for piano, like the soulful one in A major, Opus 118, No. 2,* may stimulate feelings associated with love, but the kind of love conveyed—from mother love to romantic love—depends on what you bring to it. Reexperiencing music in your body and mind is what makes it your own. This process differs from listener to listener and requires what composer Roger Sessions calls "an activity of the soul." Even if you don't know the story from Dante's *Divine Comedy*, when you hear Tchaikovsky's *Francesca da Rimini* you will recognize in the music's passion and yearning a tragic love story. Yet each of you would supply your own details. Once the psyche is aroused, as we know from dreams, it is an endlessly rich storehouse of images.

This is what listeners who look *only* outside themselves for musical meaning are missing; it is not just something external. *You* are the medium upon which music acts, and your participation is needed. It's like looking at a flower. The meaning is in our response to the flower. In *Art as Experience* John Dewey called listening "a rhythm of surrender and reflection." First, you must let yourself be enthralled by a work, then withdraw from its hypnotic effect to ask the nature of what has moved you. Music has meaning to the degree that you discover it inside.

If music didn't tell our stories, as well as those of its composer, we wouldn't be so engaged. What the G-flat Impromptu, Opus 90,* conveys with such beauty about Schubert's spiritual relationship with the world has enabled me to hear this piece over many years and still find new meaning. The way Schubert juxtaposes the lyrical beauty of the melodic line with the dark motive that rises threateningly from the bass midway through the piece suggests the inextricable nature of pain and beauty. It is as if the more beauty the music reveals, the greater the pain in losing it. Though not as encompassing as a large work like his *Unfinished Symphony,* this piece brings together opposites—life and death, good and evil, the temporal and the eternal—and holds them in tension, just as we strive to contain our inner conflicts, without forcing a resolution.

At times, a small work may communicate just the moment of vision we need. Other musical jewels, each a universe in a grain of sand, are the late works of Beethoven, the Six Bagatelles, Opus 126. The fifth in the set, "Quasi allegretto,"* is a gem that gives us a glimpse of a serene paradise. Can a piece that lasts only three minutes deepen our understanding of the true nature of the heart? This piece is my affirmative answer. After all the complications of his previous compositions, the playfulness and simplicity of this work is remarkable.

Ways of Listening

In his excellent short guide, *What to Listen for in Music,* Aaron Copland describes three different planes of listening: the sensuous, the expressive, and the sheerly musical. The sensuous refers to the passive way we hear when not listening *for* something; the expressive, to our awareness of the emotional content and mood of music; and the musical, to the intellectual observation of the structure, harmony, and style. Each listener catches onto something different, whether it is the sensuous flow or the overall structure. But to some degree everyone responds to the sensuous qualities of music: rhythm, melody, and harmony.

Of the four types of brain waves—beta, alpha, theta, and delta—beta waves are predominant in our ordinary thinking. Likewise when you are listening for the style, structure, and content of a piece. The three other frequencies are predominant in states of relaxation, meditation, and sleep. Listening to music gives rise to combinations of waves, which vary with the music and the listener, as you might expect. The right hemisphere of the brain is most active when you are appreciating the overall sense of the music, picking up the mood projected and synthesizing all the elements into a whole. It seems that the more musical training you have, the more activity there is in the left hemisphere. Following and analyzing the structure of a piece—how the composer has combined, developed, and transformed the musical materials—is primarily an activity of the left brain. But there is no simple correlation between the pleasure experienced in hearing music and your degree of training. Professional musicians, like professionals in any field, can get so caught up in the technical side of what they're doing that they forget what attracted them to it in the first place. In the end, whatever your knowledge of music, it is the pleasure it gives that draws you closer.

Some people listen to music in a physically passive, internalized way (Apollonian), perhaps visualizing architectural or spatial forms in changing relationships to one another. In the Allegro* from Bach's Brandenburg Concerto in F major, you can follow the different groups of instruments in dialogue, perhaps imagining them across the room from one another. Other people have a full-bodied response (Dionysian), feeling the music kinetically in and through the body, often wanting to move to it. Many listen both ways at once, and have other, subtle perceptions we may not have named or even identified. Because a piece like the Brahms Intermezzo in A major* follows the contours of the human heart, it may cause your breath to fluctuate, or shift your energy, perhaps making you feel lighter (or heavier).

Some music is difficult to sit still for. Gospel choirs move while they sing, which can have a contagious effect on an audience. Classical musicians are discouraged from swinging and swaying, as jazz musicians often do, because it is said to distract from the music. But most of us have seen members of symphonies or chamber groups, let alone soloists, who move quite a bit, despite the constrictions of formal training and attire. It seems that to be a channel for passionate expression involves the whole body. Watch the faces of great musicians as they mirror changing details of harmony and rhythm, and notice the eloquent hands of conductors as they shape every nuance of a musical line. To see Leonard Bernstein conduct was to know the meaning of the music. Orchestra members who worked with him said that when he was crying they felt their instruments crying, too. It was as if Bernstein had taken to heart the words in Carl Philipp Emmanuel Bach's *Essays on the True Art of Playing Keyboard Instruments*. Here, J. S. Bach's most famous son clearly spells out a philosophy that obligates a performer to interpret music in a way that touches and moves listeners:

> *A Musician cannot move others unless he too is moved. He must of necessity feel all the affects he hopes to arouse in his listener. In languishing, sad passages, he must languish and grow*

sad. Thus will the expression of the piece be more clearly per-
ceived by the audience. . . . Similarly, in lively and joyous pas-
sages the executant must again put himself in the appropriate
mood.

A dancer hearing music may see movement, a painter
may see form and color, a poet may see word images. Some
people, perhaps you are one, have a sensitivity known as
synesthesia, in which certain colors and sounds correspond.
Symbolist poets Baudelaire and Rimbaud equated vowel
sounds with specific colors, as composers Scriabin and Messaien did musical tones and colors. "A black, E white, I red,
U green," writes Rimbaud in his poem "Voyelles." Scriabin
went so far as to create a "color organ" to synthesize music
and color. It projected a color onto the screen for each note
(C was red, C sharp was violet, D was yellow, and so on). At
the end of this chapter there's an experiment that will help
you discover your own associations of color and sound.

Whatever listening style comes naturally to you, the best
attitude is one of alert openness—emotionally, psychologically, and mentally. Certainly, the more associations you
make with the music, the more alive it will be in your imagination. Margaret Mead, who was famous for remembering
practically everything she ever read or experienced, knew
how to live through all her senses. According to those who
knew her, if she were listening to music about the sea, a piece
like Debussy's *La Mer,* she would not only hear the waves

break but smell and taste the salty air and feel the sand between her toes. The more sensory neurons that are activated,
the more information the brain has with which to remember.
I like to imagine a symphony hall of the future that provides
a listening space for those who want to move more than just
the head or a foot when listening to a rollicking passage.

Tonality: The Homing Instinct

Though obvious, it's worth repeating: the ear learns to hear
sound patterns by listening, and a practiced ear perceives
more and more patterns. In earlier times a pilgrim arriving
at Chartres Cathedral would walk the labyrinth in preparation for being received into the sanctuary. Similarly, you
may need to spend time with a piece of music before you are
able to take it in fully. With each listening you pick up new
clues about how the composer has set up a theme and created
a context in which certain rhythms and harmonies can be
anticipated. And the relationships between the notes are not
just abstractions. The ear hears the energy *between* the notes,
too—as unrest, tension, or as a magnetic pull toward the
tonic or home key around which a piece is organized. With
a simple singing experiment you can experience this dynamic
between tones and the tonic's homeward pull.

Supported by a piano or by someone who can sing a
scale, try to sing in succession, *do, do re, do re mi, do re mi fa,*

and so on up the scale. Always return to *do,* the first note of any scale, to begin the upward climb. Sing these tones loudly enough to sense the growing distance separating the next (higher) tone from the original *do.* Repeat the scale and notice the feeling of half-arrival on *sol,* the fifth and most important tone after the tonic. Notice too that the further you go from *do,* the greater the expectation for a return to the stability of *do,* which is home. Now sing the opening of the Christmas carol "Joy to the World" and notice the sense of closure you feel with the the words, "the Lord is come." Do you realize that you have just sung a scale, from *do* to *do* an octave below? No combination of notes is more complete sounding than this. But the joy of leaving home—the tonic key—is equalled, or surpassed, by the joy of returning. As T. S. Eliot says in *Four Quartets,* the goal is *to arrive where we started/And know the place for the first time.*

The tonic key is king. It rules the point of departure and the point of return. The fifth tone (V) above the tonic (I), the *dominant,* is second in importance. The fourth (IV) above the tonic, the *subdominant,* is next. Harmony that has "wandered" (intentionally) away from the tonic key usually returns via the fifth tone above it. The *leading tone* (VII), however, turns the melody back to the tonic. At some point every piece of music moves inexorably toward a *cadence,* the notes or chords that give a section of music a sense of completion. But music often plays on your expectations by delaying and so increasing your desire for the final tonic. The dominant (in the key of C, for example, this would be G, five notes above C) may be drawn out interminably, heightening the dramatic tension to the maximum. In the liner notes of his set of complete Bach cello suites, Mstislav Rostropovich describes the effect of the prolonged dominant on his sensitive ears, here—in Bach's Prelude from the Unaccompanied Cello Suite No. 2—delaying the anticipated return to the tonic:

> *It's like a needle pricking the music as a lepidopterist pins a live butterfly to his board. The butterfly spins in agony around the pin, (the dominant) unable to free itself. . . . I too seem to revolve in torment on the pin, and I experience release only on return to the tonic.*

The tonic harmony has the stability of being at home, the place where we can relax. *Tonality* is this system of organizing tones, and from the time you hear your first nursery songs you develop the homing instinct for the tonic (I). And the symmetry of beginning and ending in the same place is just as gratifying in music as it is in a story.

Everyone has different tolerance levels for what is new. This affects your pleasure or displeasure when listening expectations are met or frustrated. Too little surprise can be boring; too much can be unsettling. If you are unable to anticipate correctly, at least some of the time, what the next note or chord will be, you may not be able to make sense of what you hear. This can make hearing a piece for the first time challenging, especially a modern piece whose musical vocabulary may be unfamiliar. It helps if you know what style or period to expect, although some composers such as Stravinsky, the Picasso of the music world, wrote in many styles. If you are expecting to hear his graceful, neo-classical *Apollo* or easy-on-the-ears *Pulcinella** and instead are surprised by the ecstatic but demanding *Rite of Spring,* you may not be happy. When you know that a composer's intentions are serious, that the music is well crafted, you are more willing to lend your ears. And if you come to music primarily because it calls forth from you feelings of warmth and tenderness, you need preparation before hearing strongly dissonant, strident music. On the other hand, music may be the safest possible arena for containing the conflicts that, judging from history and the repeated scenes of violence on television and movie screens, appear to be an inescapable ingredient of the human experience.

MUSIC BREAKS

Following a Line

Both kinetic and visually dominated listeners can sense the shape of a musical line by tracing it in the air. This is easy to do with pieces that have arch-shaped melodies that rise to a peak in the middle or near the end, as in many short pieces. Listen to the Chopin Mazurka, Opus 63, No. 3,* letting your hand rise and fall with the melody, registering its movement like a seismograph.

Hearing in Color

Sit down with an array of colored pencils or crayons and paper. Listen to Debussy's "Dr. Gradus as Parnassum"* from *Children's Corner,* and let the music guide you to the colors you hear in the music. Then try the same experiment while listening to Stravinsky's *Pulcinella.**

FOUR

When You Are the Music

If we bring forth that which is within us it will save us.
If we do not bring forth that which is
within us it will destroy us.

THE GOSPEL ACCORDING TO THOMAS

Your Unlived Life

Sometimes it is difficult to be just one person, while within us so many selves come and go and a great range of possibilities may lie dormant. Despite the personal and professional roles we play over a lifetime, there are times when work, marriage, family, and friends leave our hearts and spirits craving something more. Rainer Maria Rilke, in *The Notebooks of Malte Laurids Brigge*, writes of "that un-lived life of which one can die." When our lives don't seem large enough for our souls, we look to the arts, to fiction, drama, and music—for reflections of our many facets.

Because music engages us on so many levels, it can animate aspects of the soul that may need to be acknowledged. At day's end a social worker or psychologist who has been dealing with emotional conflicts may be drawn to music that feels spacious, cool, and ordered, rather than highly emotional—Debussy's "The Maiden with the Flaxen Hair" * or a longer work, *Prelude to the Afternoon of a Faun*. A computer scientist who has spent the day with abstract problems may crave heartwarming, expressive music—the Andante* from Schubert's Piano Sonata in A major, Op. 120, his Impromptu in G-flat, Opus 90,* or Brahms's Intermezzo in A major, Opus 118, No. 2.* And there is certainly a time and a place for cathartic music, as I'll discuss in chapter 7. Music can bring whatever qualities we desire into our daily reality, and this is especially redeeming in an environment that is deficient. The yearning for expression, like the yearning for love, can be limitless. "Oh the fabulous wings unused, folded in the heart," wrote dramatist Christopher Fry. Music allows us to spread our wings, even when they may be protecting tender, vulnerable places.

One mark of great music is its ability to animate contradictions that may lie dormant and unexplored within us. Yin and yang, feminine and masculine, passive and active, violent and tender—opposites not only exist but may unite in music, and with less difficulty than they do in reality. Carl

Jung asserted that oppositions constitute the basic anatomy of the psyche and that to unify them is our essential task. "Without Contraries is no progression," said William Blake in *The Marriage of Heaven and Hell*. Internal contradictions can tear us apart without a model of expression and containment such as music.

Before turning to Bach and Beethoven and what their music brings alive in us, I want to touch briefly on how the music of Richard Wagner explores instincts and passions that could be destructive if expressed in actions. His operas are dramas in which powerful energies are tried, tested, and often transformed. In music that goes beyond ideology, Wagner depicts competing claims of power, love, and allegiance. There is the myth of the heroic knight who goes on a quest and is tested by challenges along the way (Parsifal and Siegfried). In the Ring cycle Wagner treats the taboo of incest between brother and sister, Siegmund and Sieglinde, giving musical form to repressed instincts and primitive urges. The sensual and spiritual yearnings conveyed through such music can stir listeners almost as deeply as dreams. They stimulate not only the personal but the collective unconscious, that storehouse of common, cultural memory that Jung believed influences our lives subterraneously. In harmonies as chromatically close and complex (because they use clashing adjacent notes) as the ties of blood and loyalty that bind one character to another, Wagner translates eroticism into surging, undulating sounds that seem to invite us . . . we know not where. It's easy to get carried away in trying to describe the Wagner experience. The rise and fall of the love duet in *Tristan and Isolde* can seduce the senses with a force the intellect alone cannot grasp. With thick, dark chords that don't resolve but become an ongoing stream of unrelieved longing, Wagner draws us into the magic circle of the ill-fated lovers. As in Shakespeare's *Romeo and Juliet,* values are turned upside down; the day world becomes the enemy of love and the night its friend. Wagner's music reminds us that half our lives are lived in darkness, and that we are not intellect alone. Yet in contrast to the sensuality of *Tristan,* the music of the Grail in *Lohengrin* and in the Good Friday episode in *Parsifal* is ascetic and restrained. It has the sound of grace descending, quiet and numinous. If music is large enough to hold the contradictions that are Richard Wagner, it can hold your own.

Because music comes to the secret self, the inner knower who shapes and guides the soul, no two listeners will have the same experience. Writing about the way we hear, Zuckerkandl writes that the ear is like "a hand the inner life holds out to outer life." It receives, welcomes, and confirms our being. When music matches our need, it brings the comfort of feeling understood at the deepest level, where even close relationships sometimes fail us. Unique parts of the self that find no connection with others may find a place in a piece of music. Consider the melancholy mood, which our culture encourages us not to impose on others. One of the four hu-

mors—along with the choleric, the sanguine, and the phlegmatic—melancholy was once regarded as a constant part of
the soul, a muse to artists, and a friend of intellectuals. It
could inspire insights and ideas. Shakespeare's Hamlet is the
supreme example of this type. When given expression in
music, melancholy can even be savored. In a culture that
puts such a high value on efficiency and productivity, we
deny sad feelings in part because they slow us down. But
consider how much great poetry, art, and music has been
seeded and ripened by that contraction of attention we call
a melancholy mood. Are there any aspects of the human experience that can't find some form in music? According to
Proust there need not be:

> . . . the field open to the musician is not a miserable stave of
> seven notes, but an immeasurable keyboard (still, almost all of
> it, entirely unknown) on which . . . some few among the mil-
> lions of keys, keys of tenderness, of passion, of courage, of
> serenity, which compose it, each one differing from all the rest
> as one universe differs from another, have been discovered by a
> few great artists . . . [1]

For Gustav Mahler, to write a symphony was to
construct a world, a chance to create a more truthful, beautiful, and complete world than that of his last work. In
Beethoven's case, each major work ventures into a different
corner of his mind and heart. And as Beethoven was led

more deeply into himself, so he is able to lead us. In the popular, nicknamed sonatas of his middle period, including the Pathétique (Opus 13), Moonlight (Opus 27, No. 2), Waldstein (Opus 54), and Appassionata (Opus 57), Beethoven experimented with form and content. Each work has a unique character. Once he had solved a particular compositional problem, he would challenge himself with another. Through his music, Beethoven expressed contradictions in his personality that had damaging effects when played out in relationships, such as the troubled ones with his brother's wife and her son Karl, the nephew for whom Beethoven fought a five-year custody battle after the death of the boy's father. Convinced that he would be a more positive influence on the young man's education than Karl's mother, Beethoven set unrealistically high expectations for his nephew that may have contributed to Karl's attempted suicide.

But Beethoven's music is not always the quality of energy or inspiration we seek. Sometimes we must go outside our cultural tradition to find the kind and quality of expression we desire—as many composers have done. And because nothing gives voice to the spirit of a culture better than its music, it may be the ideal form of armchair travel. Today, as never before, we can hear music, and fusions of music, from almost every country in the world. New music can open up new realities.

This was the effect on Debussy of hearing exotic music from Spain and Indonesia at the Paris Exposition of 1900.

I've already referred to the way the new timbres and harmonic colors of the Indonesian gamelan orchestra showed him a new palette of sound color. In the Spanish music Debussy was drawn to, the Moorish elements particularly fertilized his imagination. And if you doubt that music can carry the spirit of a culture, listen to Debussy's amazingly idiomatic Spanish music, piano pieces like "La Puerta del Vino" and "Soirée dans Grenade" and *Iberia* for orchestra, and remember that the composer spent only a few hours in Spain, in the Basque town of San Sebastián. In "La Puerta del Vino," named for the place where the Gypsies traditionally meet in Granada, Debussy incorporates the vocal arabesques and wailing sound of *cante jondo*—the deep song of Andalusia, an ancient form of the blues. He suggests first a sultry and then a violent mood by superimposing harmonies from two different keys. Debussy's culturally enriched sound was so original that Stravinsky, a master of orchestral color himself, said that it was Debussy who taught him how to hear.

It is possible to extend a trip once you return home, as I once did after visiting Spain, by playing Granados's *Spanish Dances* and pieces by Albeniz, de Falla, and Mompou. Full of the atmosphere of the bull ring and the spirit of flamenco, this music mingles sensual Andalusian dances with the Arab-African, early Jewish, and Christian roots of Spanish music. And I never tire of Bizet's great opera *Carmen*, which captures the stark contrasts of masculine machismo and feminine sensuality in Spanish culture. An evening with *Carmen* is a cathartic experience where all the complex emotions between the sexes are played out—love, hate, desire, jealousy, and dominance.

Music makes expression possible, even of aspects of the self that may be repressed because they are unacceptable to the rational mind. With its capacity to bridge conscious and unconscious levels of being, music can give form to imprecise, vague feelings that are only half-conscious. Artists, as Jung pointed out, have a more permeable partition between the conscious and unconscious worlds. Late in life Socrates had a dream that instructed him to study music, which he did. After a lifetime of cultivating rational discourse, his soul was asking for another kind of expression.

Bach: The Passionate Mind

We begin with Johann Sebastian Bach, the ancestor of all music that has succeeded him. So central is Bach to the Baroque period, which preceded the Classic period of Mozart and Haydn, that the year of his death, 1750, is generally considered the boundary for the end of the period. The greatest music can arise only when all the tones and harmonies of what it means to be human come together in an artist, as they do in Bach. When the poet Walt Whitman wrote, "I am large. I contain multitudes," he might have been describing Bach. Legendary cellist Pablo Casals called Bach "a volcano" of creativity. He was referring to the way Bach's compositions comprise a full spectrum of expression: classic and romantic, abstract and pictorial, traditional and original, introspective and impersonal. "[Bach] is like Shakespeare in that every work is a self-portrait, yet he himself remains an enigma."[2] Bach is one of the few great artists who left behind no biographical writings, but his music made his artistic creed clear. It reflects the attitude prevalent through the Middle Ages—art exists to praise God. Bach inscribes his religious scores with the letters J. J. (*Jesu, Juva:* "Jesus, help") at the beginning and S.D.G. (*Soli Deo Gloria:* "to God alone the glory") at the end. For the Lutheran branch of the Protestant church, Bach composed over 170 cantatas, yet like Martin Luther, he knew that instrumental music could be spiritual, too. Some movements of Bach's unaccompanied suites for cello are as profound as his church music.

More than three hundred years after Bach's birth in 1685, his music is still demanding. Playing Bach at the keyboard is to feel the mind, body, and emotional system engaged at once; there is no choice but total commitment and concentration. Superior intelligence and magnanimity, together with an unparalleled mastery of craft and an unwavering faith, are the roots of Bach's legacy. His music affirms the goodness of creation even as it acknowledges the presence of tragedy and sorrow. Bach knows what Rilke knows when he writes in the eighth *Sonnet to Orpheus* that grief should walk only in the footsteps of praise, for joy already understands what grief is still learning—life is to be praised. Bach communicates this understanding through the inevitability of his cadences; their rightness brings repose and a sense of fulfillment.

Whatever he suffered in his personal life, in his musical life Bach remained disciplined and productive. Orphaned by the age of ten, a husband to two wives and father to twenty children, Bach had more than his share of human troubles. He even had to answer for debts incurred by one of his gifted sons who drank too much and borrowed money. Yet Bach left behind a tremendous volume of music, a masterpiece in almost every genre. He was quite simply a master of everything he touched. Visualize almost two yards of music in compact disc jewel boxes. This is the space required for Bach's recently issued complete works, numbering 153 discs. And all this in a lifespan of sixty-five years.

As a young man, Bach walked 200 miles to hear the great Buxtehude play the organ. A spirited, strong-willed man, Sebastian, as he was called, could lose his temper, and did, in a famous street brawl with a student. He was even imprisoned for a month when he left a musical post for one more advantageous. The year that he wrote the dramatic *Chromatic Fantasy and Fugue* for keyboard and the great Second Partita in D minor for violin, with its famous Chaconne movement, Bach returned from a trip to find that his young wife had died during his absence. Some commentators think that the intense, riveting Chaconne—a kind of death dance with a glimpse of heaven in the middle—is his personal requiem for his wife. In the expressive extremes of these works, with notes so rapid at times that they seem out of control, we can hear Bach's struggle to order and master tremendous passion. This music is a model for containment and true expression of emotions that, unfocused, might be disruptive, possibly destructive.

In Bach's music the frequent sequences of repeated melodic and rhythmic patterns we expect in Baroque music are clear and usually easy to pick up. They give your ear a structural design it can follow like a path, as you can hear in the Little Prelude in C* and in the Fugue.* Perhaps more frequently than his brilliant contemporaries, Vivaldi and Scarlatti, Bach takes turns that keep us alert and surprised. You might think of the six *Brandenburg Concerti* as a Baroque jam session, the way different instruments take the spotlight (in one the recorders are soloists, in another the flute, violin, or harpsichord). More often Bach delights rather than confuses us, for there is always the reassuring design, beginning, middle, and return to the beginning, that *New York Times* music critic Bernard Holland dubs "an emotional round-trip ticket."

The energy and optimism in Bach's music can be particularly stabilizing when your own life feels confused or uncertain. In teaching Bach to volatile teenagers (not to mention in managing my own highs and lows) I have seen the steadying effect of his music, its amazing ability to smooth ragged emotions and put the soul in order. Instead of trying to organize a desk or closet, as you might do when the larger patterns of your life are disturbed or threatened, you can listen to Bach's *Two and Three Part Inventions* for the clarity and comfort of their ordered design. Music like this places you within a context larger than the merely personal. And the spirit of Bach's music is not confined to the solemnity of a Sunday meditation—in Cantata BWV 31, he composes music to the words "The Heavens Laugh." And before the repetition of the sublime aria in the *Goldberg Variations*, in Variation 30, Bach quotes an earthy drinking song about the odors of kale and cabbage.

Although Bach's emotional mountains and valleys are sometimes steep, as in his account of the scourging and crucifixion of Jesus in the *St. Matthew Passion*, he gives us comfort and continuity by scattering twelve four-part chorales throughout the *Passion*. The steady tempo of these chorales reassures us that life goes on. Bach is always the good shepherd, responsive and attendant to our needs. If you long to drop into a place of inner peace, you can be carried by the steady, flowing tempo of "Jesu, Joy of Man's Desiring" from Cantata No. 147. And the well-loved air from the Orchestra Suite No. 3 in D major, BWV 1068, can always be counted on to put the heart at rest. Many of us have been supported during difficult times by the dignity such music gives to feeling. The healthy resilience of Bach's spirit can be as warming as a great fire on a winter night. And is there better music for the end of life than the cantata, *Actus tragicus* (BWV 106), *God's Time Is the Best Time?*

It has been said that from Bach's music alone, future composers could have derived all that has followed. The seeds of Western music lie in the preludes and fugues of his two-volume keyboard work, *The Well-Tempered Clavier,* a kind of Old and New Testament for keyboard players. Robert Schumann called *The Well-Tempered Clavier* the musician's daily bread, and Casals said it gave him a pattern for living. Goethe expressed his stunned response to his first hearing of these preludes and fugues this way: "It was as though eternal harmony conversed with itself . . . shortly before the creation of the world." Though we know him as a cellist, when Casals was so crippled with arthritis that he had trouble dressing, he continued to sit at the piano every morning and play two or three preludes and fugues. In *Anatomy of an Illness,* Norman Cousins describes how he watched Casals's clenched hands miraculously begin to relax as they moved over the keys. Another admirer of Bach, Otto Bettmann, founder of the photo archive and author of a book on Bach, found that listening to Bach's music helped him get through his daily push-ups because Bach's energy catalyzed his own.

So deeply rooted in faith was Bach that even his grief could become a song and in the singing be transformed.

Casals's recording of Bach's Sixth Unaccompanied Cello Suite No. 6 inspired poet Howard Nemerov, and he must have been speaking of the Sarabande when he wrote:

> *Deep in a time that cannot come again*
> *Bach thought it through, this lonely and immense*
> *Reflexion wherein our sorrows learn to dance.*[3]

Listening to Bach's suites and partitas for keyboard or for cello or violin is a way of enlarging our conversation with the world. Mountains and rivers, clouds and continents, the moon and stars, all feel present in these works. It is the whole cosmos Bach seems to embrace, not just the human world, viewed from a perspective that recognizes the unity of life. If music alone could make us better people, this music surely would.

Beethoven: A Guide to Spiritual Evolution

> *Joy, beautiful spark of the gods,*
> *Daughter of Elysium,*
> *Intoxicated with fire we enter*
> *Thy sanctuary, heavenly being.*

Your magic spell reunites
What custom has torn apart . . .

Why do so many of us love the opera? What touches us in the fervent arias of Violetta, Alfredo, Tosca, and Cavaradossi as they sing out their delight and grief, rapture and despair? Even death can be an occasion for exalting love and faithfulness, as in the last scene of Verdi's *Aïda,* when the lovers sing farewell to life, "O addio, terra," from their tomb. We may long to have loves worthy of arias by Puccini or Verdi, but do we dare express our desires so ardently? Had we more courage, were we more great-hearted (*courage* derives from the same word as *heart*), wouldn't we live more operatically, more poetically, and risk all for love? Emotional excitement has enough positive value that we go to great lengths to seek it out. Hector Berlioz, it is said, once wept through an entire concert, then turned to the man seated next to him and explained, "You don't think I came here for pleasure do you?" Without passion to stir our hearts and imaginations, life would seem a pale reflection of what it could be.

The genesis of opera in the Baroque era was the most important musical event of the last four hundred years. In the sixteenth century the desire for greater expression led composers of madrigals (secular songs) to increasing extremes and exaggerations in word painting. Still, the sentiment grew that the many voices of a madrigal ensemble could not express human feeling as strongly as a single human voice, a great singer who could use techniques learned from actors and orators to move an audience to tears or to laughter. This set the scene for the gradual development of opera through the seventeenth and eighteenth centuries, and on to the early nineteenth century, with the *bel canto* (beautiful song) of Italian opera composers Rossini, Donizetti, and Bellini. Later in the nineteenth century would come the great Giuseppe Verdi.

Besides clearing the way for the symphony and concerto, opera prepared the ground for Beethoven. His direct and passionate expression of emotion has an operatic intensity that can be extroverted in his symphonies and deeply introverted in his late piano sonatas and string quartets. We think of Beethoven now as the prototype of the artist as a revolutionary figure, a challenger of the prevailing order. He was that, too, but it's more accurate to think of him as the transitional figure who spanned the Classic period of Mozart and Haydn and that of the early Romantics Schubert, Mendelssohn, Chopin, Schumann, and Liszt. His early works follow the example of Haydn and Mozart; his middle period includes the "heroic" works such as the *Eroica* and the Fifth Symphonies; and his third period refers to the works of his last decade.

We owe our basic ideas about what art can and should be more to Beethoven and the Romantic generation that followed than to the comparatively objective music of the

Baroque and Classic periods. Since Beethoven, we've come to expect a composer, or any artist, to take his fears, hang-ups, and conflicts and work them out through his art. Over the course of the four movements of Beethoven's Fifth Symphony, for example, he does something musicologist Joseph Kerman says is "novel in the instrumental music of his or any earlier time." From the opening four notes, "There Fate knocks at the door!" as Beethoven is supposed to have said about this theme, until Fate is trampled under in defeat by a military march in the last movement, the symphony dramatically traces a psychological progression through its various stages. That so many listeners have been able to understand and follow this life process, and to find it inspiring, is proof of Beethoven's greatness as a communicator and to the universality of his spiritual search. The glory of his symphonies and sonatas is that the conflicts presented in the first movement are resolved by the end of the work. This satisfies our need for a reality-based model that includes difficulties to be faced and assurances that they will be surmounted.

His correspondence and *Tagebuch* (Daybook) entries trace his spiritual evolution: from the proud defiance of his youth ("I will take Fate by the throat") to his resistance to the onset of deafness ("I have often cursed my Creator") and finally his submission to what he came to accept as his fate. He exhorts himself over and over to "endure." In the String Quartet, Opus 135, Beethoven writes on the score of the finale the words "Must it be?" The sheaves of messy, ink-spattered pages on which he worked out compositions that now strike us as miraculous testify to the ongoing work-in-progress that characterizes Beethoven. Genius aside, his road, like many of ours, was full of detours and rough spots. And it may be this all-too-human aspect of Beethoven that draws us in. As high as he reaches toward joy and peaceful acceptance—in the "Ode to Joy" of the Ninth Symphony, the sublime slow movement of the Emperor Concerto, and the numinous Cavatina* from the Quartet in B-flat, Opus 130—Beethoven's feet were never entirely free of mud. He continually had to tame and sublimate the energy of the wild, awkward aspects of his temperament. And this struggle to rise above is what we hear in his music. Beethoven shows us that, with effort, we can redeem what is unrefined, coarse, and ungenerous in our personality.

Perhaps no other composer's music embraces so many contrasts as Beethoven's. There are tender movements when he seems to be caressing your cheek—in the spacious themes of slow movements such as the Piano Sonata, Opus 13 (the Pathétique) or the Trio in B-flat, Opus 97 (the Archduke). When a rare breakdown occurs in Beethoven's speech, as in the halting, broken-off phrases of the Arioso movement of the Piano Sonata No. 31, Opus 110, it is more expressive than fluency could ever be. A pianist friend of mine once commented, "If Beethoven can live with these contradictions I guess I can live with mine." To hear both the sublime and the crabbed Beethoven we have only to listen to the Lento from the String Quartet in F, Opus 135, alongside the strident theme of the Grosse Fugue (Great Fugue) movement of the late quartet, Opus 133. Transcending barriers was a theme of the Romantic period, and it is Beethoven's gift. As Stravinsky said, the Grosse Fugue will always be modern.

The strength and determination of Beethoven's character translate musically into a tremendous rhythmic drive and the consistency with which he works on motives like the one that opens the Fifth Symphony, staying with it until, like a seed, it sprouts leaves and branches. When our courage needs strengthening, this is music we can turn to. For Beethoven, life demanded that his vision expand to include more and, at the same time, that his introspection deepen. Certainly his growing deafness helped drive him inward. We listen to his late string quartets, which are both private and public, as if we were eavesdropping on a self-absorbed dialogue with the divine. Like his other late works, they point the way from the isolation of individual passion to a compassionate unity with others. If he had not been a composer, might he have been a great theologian? Aaron Copland writes:

Beethoven is one of the great yea-sayers among creative artists . . . His music summons forth our better nature; in purely musical terms he seems to be exhorting us to Be Noble, Be Strong, Be Great in Heart, yes, and Be Compassionate.

But the contrasts in Beethoven's music demand more elasticity in your attitude than when listening to Bach or Mozart. Beethoven is more likely to bounce you abruptly from the reflective depths of a slow movement like the numinous one in the Piano Concerto No. 5 (the Emperor) into a fast Vivace or Presto. You must be fast on your feet, flexible, and willing to jump into the next mood even before you're ready. Listening to Beethoven's slow movements as gratefully as I do, I always want to linger there longer. An older pianist I know now plays *only* the slow movements, those marked Largo, Adagio, and Andante. It is hard to believe that the same man who wrote the furious first movements of the Third and Fifth Symphonies was also capable of the tenderness we hear in the first movements of the piano sonatas No. 12 in A-flat (Opus 26) and No. 18 in E-flat (Opus 31, No. 3). Like Chagall's lovers, Beethoven longed to leave the earth.

After all, as one of the first generation of composer-pianists to grow up with what was close to a modern piano, Beethoven was well positioned historically as well as temperamentally to enlarge the range and the treatment of the keyboard. Beginning with Opus 57 (the Appasionata), he writes passages in his piano sonatas that are symphonic in concept, as if straining for the sound of a whole orchestra. In the conclusion of his final sonata, No. 32, Opus 111, he separates the player's hands as far as possible from each other to span a greater range of sound. Beethoven was also the first to explore the magic of the damper pedal. In the Rondo of Piano Sonata, Opus 53 (the Waldstein), he indicates that the pedal be depressed for eight bars, to imitate the blurred din of ringing bells.

Like Mahler, Beethoven was more productive during the warmer months, when he would take long walks in the countryside around Vienna. "It seems as if in the country every tree said to me 'Holy! Holy!' " You can hear this worshipful attitude toward the beauty of the natural world so clearly in his Sixth Symphony (the Pastorale). This is wonderful music to pop into your Walkman when you venture out into the kind of setting that inspired it: meadows, trees, mountains, and sky. The exuberance of the final movement, which Beethoven called "Joyous thanksgiving after the storm," is greater because of the preceding thunderous eruption. Experiencing this symphony can be a cathartic journey, marking the reaffirmation of faith and hope. Its alchemy seldom fails to transform a dark mood. Who can resist being uplifted in the presence of so much exultation?

One event stands out in Beethoven's personal life—and also marked his music. That was his love for the woman whom biographer Maynard Solomon persuasively argues was the noblewoman Antonie Brentano. Consummated or not, love can shelter the most tender feelings, yet no power can be more galvanizing. The "Immortal Beloved" letters coincide with the end of his heroic period, which includes the Third (*Eroica*) and the Fifth Symphonies, and the beginning of his late period. Solomon argues that Beethoven's love for Antonie Brentano left him changed, catalyzing the development of his more organic works that followed. His music becomes more introspective and freer in form, with an improvised quality, as in the first movement of the Piano Sonata No. 31, Opus 110. It seems the heroism of late Beethoven was of an *inner* nature.

No work better summarizes this period for Beethoven than the Piano Trio in B-flat, Opus 97 (the Archduke). It was completed just before the intense crisis in his affair (or possibly non-affair) with Brentano. Beethoven's love had not been returned in kind until his love for this married friend flared into the passion expressed in a letter found after his death. "Is not our love truly a heavenly structure, and also as firm as the vault of Heaven?" he writes. The opening movement has the noble sweep and grandeur of earlier heroic works, but the slow Andante movement looks forward to the profound world of the later string quartets. With its broad, lush lyricism, this movement, a theme with variations, is the emotional center of the Archduke, and it is Beethoven's love letter to Antonie. The form is based on a standard technique in which note values become smaller with each variation *(diminution)*, adding a sense of speed and excitement. The surprise is the almost hedonistic world of sensuous beauty Beethoven miraculously creates with this technique.

But the most famous movement in Beethoven's chamber works is in the late quartets, the Molto Adagio, "Thanksgiving" movement of the Quartet in A minor, Opus 132. This was his song of gratitude to God after recovering from a serious illness. No one who is receptive to the contemplative spirit of this movement can fail to be moved by it. Like Jacob wrestling with the angel, Beethoven always struggles until he is blessed. What he finally comes to understand is that his suffering is necessary to his unique expression of the extremes of joy and despair.

It is not to some unattainable perfection that Beethoven's music seems to call us. He challenges us to rise to our own highest nature as human beings. As his hearing faded, he seemed to have developed a deep inner hearing. One gift of this period is the spiritual world of the Cavatina* from the late Quartet in B-flat (Opus 130). Beethoven confessed to his friend Karl Holz that he never heard this serenely beautiful fragment of music without tears. As Beethoven grew older, he longed to touch the infinite—"Seek Him above the stars," are the words of Schiller that Beethoven set in the Ninth Symphony. This work expresses his desire to embrace all humanity, and the history of performances of the Ninth have born out this hope. It was the work chosen to celebrate both the fall of the Berlin Wall and the beginning of the new millennium.

A performance of the Ninth is a communal event. Leonard Bernstein, whose recording of the Ninth is considered one of the most completely realized, said that to perform this work in the spirit it was intended requires a full acceptance of "the pure simplicity of [Beethoven's] childlike belief," when the score cries out "Brother," "Joy," and "God."

Praise and Prayer

There is a tale from Greek antiquity in which Zeus, having made the world, calls together the gods to show them his work. The gods admire the world in silence. When Zeus asks if anything is missing they answer, "Your work is great and glorious, but the voice that would praise this great work is missing." And so Zeus, together with Mnemosyne (Memory), brought the nine Muses into being to praise creation through the arts. Creative artists continue to invoke the Muses as a source of inspiration—even though Christianity transferred the source of creativity from them to God.

Listening to songs of praise, from Hildegard of Bingen's to Bach's to Messaien's, are a way we can restore our connection with the divine. In Judaism, prayers are always sung, for song is thought to be the only fitting language for the divine. To hear or play the music you love can be a form of prayer; like a mantra, praise music drives deeper a certain state of being. After listening to a favorite piece of music, you may feel the air resonate with presences and possibilities. No silence is fuller than that which follows music.

Hildegard, the extraordinary twelfth-century abbess, writer, artist, and composer, viewed her music as a reminiscence of the angels' songs. Regarding herself as an instrument, "a feather on the breath of God," she created devotional music for her abbey on the Rhine that is stunning for her time and for ours. With sinuous melodies that range over two octaves and elaborate *melismas* (segments of melody that are sung on a single syllable), this music can change one's orientation. Listening to her "Ave Generosa,"* as I often do driving the country road from my home to the freeway, I am more likely to marvel at the beauty of the light on the leaves or the shapes of clouds. Instead of rushing toward a goal, oblivious to what is around, I am brought into the exquisite reality of the moment. I drive more carefully wrapped in this blessed sound cocoon because I feel more connected with other living things.

Among the greatest music of praise ever written are the choral works of Flemish masters such as Josquin des Pres, Giovanni Pierluigi da Palestrina, and Orlando di Lasso. Their *polyphonic* texture, that is, where two or more voices are sung simultaneously, gives them the many-colored richness of a tapestry. When music is joined to a text of praise, as it is in Palestrina's "Gloria," the effect can be transcendental—the kind of sound we imagine coming from the music-making angels in early Italian paintings. In his *Pope*

Marcellus Mass of 1555 Palestrina is said to have saved church music from abolition by Pope Marcellus, the head of the Church at that time, by setting an example of clarity, demonstrating that the meaning of the words was not lost within a complex polytonal texture. Waking in the morning to this music is like being sung from your dreams by a heavenly chorus. It sets a tone of gratitude for the day. The *Upanishads* say, "Because I sang praises, I became joyful," but it works both ways: we sing because we're joyful and singing brings joy. Why do so many psalms begin with "Praise ye the Lord"? They are pointing us toward happiness by reinforcing an attitude of gratitude.

When you love music, its existence is both a cause for praise and the *vehicle* for it. Like grace, joy can surprise you. In fact joy, like rapture, may be the greatest component of our unlived lives—and it comes unsought, when you have forgotten yourself. The rapturous conclusion of the Ninth Symphony's "Ode to Joy," like that of the "Gloria" in Bach's B minor Mass, reminds us that, lived or unlived, feared or pursued, joy is us! And when you are feeling gratitude you are not suffering. "Knowledge of the ecstatic states comes through the music of Bach and Beethoven," says pianist Keith Jarrett, whose own ecstatic musical experience was recorded in a seventy-minute improvisation, the Köln Concert, certainly one of the most remarkable jazz performances. To reach beyond personality is to touch the divine, as Beethoven came to know. That music can evoke a greater reality is the secret of its healing power, and living in relation to something greater than ourselves is the essence of prayer. Saint Teresa spoke of "prayer without ceasing," and Thomas Merton wanted a prayerful connection "with everything I touch." Poet Alla Renée Bozarth believes that anything we do can be prayer:

> *Learn and play your prayer,*
> *work and rest your prayer,*
> *fast and feast your prayer,*
> *argue, talk, whisper, listen and shout your prayer,*
> *groan and moan and spit and sneeze your prayer,*
> *swim and hunt and cook your prayer,*
> *digest and become your prayer,*
> *release and recover your prayer,*
> *breathe your prayer,*
> *be your prayer.* [4]

MUSIC BREAKS

Moving to Music

Let the clear beats of the Allegro* and Andante* movements of Bach's Brandenburg Concerto in

F major move you—to walking, running, or dancing. Now try to listen without moving any part of the body. Is that difficult?

Living the Music

Listen to Bach's Sarabande from the Unaccompanied Cello Suite No. 6, inspirational music that touches the soul. As you listen to its passionate expression, imagine that you are holding the cello in one hand and the bow in the other. Make any movements or gestures that help the music come through you, as if you alone were creating it.

Opening to Joy

If you've not heard it recently, or ever, set aside seventy minutes to experience Beethoven's Ninth Symphony without interruption. Turn off the phone, close the door, and allow yourself to be transported. As you follow the movement of the music through darkness and confusion into light and affirmation, you will find yourself in a world where everything seems larger than life. The slashing kettledrums at the beginning of the Scherzo (second movement) are a stark contrast to the gossamer otherworldliness of the third movement Adagio. An hour into the fourth movement, when the glorious theme of the "Ode to Joy" is first taken up by the chorus, you will be gripped, no matter how many times you may have heard it, with a tremendous anticipation for the radiant finale that has become a symbol for freedom and brotherhood.

Blessing the Day

❈

Dim the lights, stretch out, and listen to the Cavatina* from Beethoven's String Quartet in B-flat (Opus 130), an affirmation of gratitude that is a prayer. Let the sweetness in this music be a soothing balm to a place in your life where healing is needed.

Paradise Remembered

❈

As you listen to Hildegard's "Ave Generosa,"* enjoy the exuberance of the music, with its wide leaps of fifths and octaves and long phrases that singers say can induce the natural high of hyperventilation. Let yourself synchronize with the sounds until its spirit and harmony become your own. Allow your heart to expand into its boundless nature. When the music ends, sit in silence with whatever echoes in you.

FIVE

Singing Your Own Song

Today, like every other day, we wake up empty
and frightened. Don't open the door to the study
and begin reading. Take down a musical instrument.

Let the beauty we love be what we do.
There are hundreds of ways to kneel and kiss the ground.

RUMI / BARKS[1]

When we're happy it's natural to sing or hum, or whoop and holler and wake up the neighborhood with a barbaric yodel. Joy wants to find a sound. Like the birds, we don't sing because we have an answer but because we have a song. When we overhear children playing contentedly by themselves, they're often singing a little song they know or one they've just made up. I remember our two-year-old daughter in the bath crooning, "I'm me, I'm me, so happy to be me." It's no different when we're unhappy or in pain. We vocalize—sigh, moan, groan, cry out—to release feeling. Making sounds is a way to commune with ourselves, bridging the distance between what we feel inside and what is outside.

I'll never forget attending a master class given by a famous vocal coach. He began by quoting these lines from a poem by Wallace Stevens which captures the singer's mystical sense of being the center of a world created by her singing:

> It was her voice that made
> The sky acutest at its vanishing.
> She measured to the hour its solitude.
> She was the single artificer of the world
> In which she sang. And when she sang, the sea,
> Whatever self it had, became the self
> That was her song, for she was the maker . . .[2]

Sound is the primary way we communicate that we're alive. We wait eagerly for a baby's first cry. We strain to hear a dying friend's last words. References to the presence of sound at the time of creation are universal. According to the Book of John, "In the beginning was the *word,*" sometimes translated as, "In the beginning was the *sound.*" In both Oceanic and Hindu creation myths, the beginning of life was a hum or vibration.[3] In both the Talmud and the cosmology of the Peruvian Indians of the Andes, the sun makes musical sounds as it rises.[4] Many indigenous traditions have regarded song as having magical power over the invisible forces that bring things into being.

So, are you ready to make yourself heard? If you merely read this chapter you may gain head knowledge but will miss a full-body experience. These experiments can be fun, and powerful, if you're willing to try. You may want some privacy, though. I'm not going to suggest that you climb on your rooftop and sing loudly, as Sufi poet Rumi encourages—not yet. Your car is one of the best places to practice vocalizing; it's a resonant chamber that magnifies sound. As you drive the freeway, only you will hear yourself humming, toning, or blithely warbling. The shower, famously, is another good resonating chamber for vocal therapy—the singing, groaning, shouting, and other vocal ablutions that help us get things off our chests, or ease regrets about things said or done, or *not* said or done.

Using the voice to release tension comes naturally to the body and is forgotten only as we become "civilized." Babies and small children are not shy about expressing their needs through sound. And in the not-too-distant past, before we became spectators at the performances of others, we raised our voices together to the gods, the sun, the moon, whatever powers we sensed in the world. Our bodies seem to have retained this memory; think of the way they discharge anxiety and tension in spontaneous sighs and moans, especially under stress. In *The Immune Power Personality*,

Henry Dreher concludes from his study of the immune system that the key to mind-body health is not avoidance of stress but development of personal techniques that increase our ability to cope with it. The vocal techniques in this chapter address this need. Notice their effects, and if anyone asks what you're doing, just tell them you're preparing for the Metropolitan Opera auditions.

Always begin by breathing deeply. One secret of why singing and vocalizing lift the spirit is that they encourage freer, fuller breathing. This, singers tell us, brings a natural high. When you wake in the morning, allow yourself a big, yawning stretch and let it become a moan or groan as you listen to the vowels hidden in your sounds. Play with the *Oh*'s and *Ah*'s, trying them at different pitches—high and low, loud and soft—observing where in your body the sound brings more release, or more aliveness. Let go of any tightness in your abdomen. If your sounds lead into a song, great. Be spontaneous. And if you live with pets, don't be surprised if they want to sing along with you.

Humming is a wonderful way to begin a morning meditation. It brings us to attention, in the same way that chanting or bell-ringing is used in monasteries. Hearing the voice and feeling its vibration clears the mind and intensifies a sense of presence. When else to hum? In airplanes, in New York taxis, in Asian bicycle rickshaws (more loudly when you feel your safety is in peril), and whenever there's a need to soothe yourself (or the driver). Even humming silently is comforting; try it before a difficult business meeting or a stressful doctor's appointment.

Nowhere have the potent energies of sound and the human voice been better understood than in India, where Buddhist and Hindu chants and mantras exist for every occasion and purpose. Each has different energetic nuances associated with a certain emotional state, depending on the order and combination of vowels and syllables. Long sounds, *Oh* and *Ah* (Allah, Yahweh, Krishna, Shiva) open the mouth and throat in an expression of awe. They are reverential, calming, and soothing. The short sounds, *e* and *i*, are shrill and excited, more energizing. When *Om mane padme hum* is chanted as a prayer to protect and bless, its long vowels assuage fear and free-floating anxiety. In the combination of short and long vowel sounds, *Kyrie eleison*, from the Christian mass, can be used as a mantra; you can hear the imploring quality of its meaning, *Lord have mercy on me*. In *Autobiography of a Yogi*, Yogananda calls mantras "instruments of thought . . . each one representing one aspect of creation. . . ." Because each of the fifty or more letters that comprise the Sanskrit alphabet has its own vibratory energy, it is a language that registers not just in the head but also in the body. George Bernard Shaw lamented that because our limited twenty-six-letter alphabet is unable to bear the burden of the range of sounds that makes Sanskrit such a perfect language, we should adopt a new alphabet with forty-two characters.[5]

When I first heard the Sanskrit *Om* chanted, I heard it as *home*. After learning more about Indian religions I realized *home* was not such a bad translation. *Om* or *Aum* is considered by Hindus and Buddhists to be the holiest of the sacred sound mantras; the *Upanishads* regard it as the seed-syllable of the universe and the beginning of all other mantras. When begun in the back of the throat, *Om* includes all the vowels in its sound. If you wanted to use just one mantra, an excellent choice would be *Om mane padme hum,* referring to the jewel at the heart of the universe. The sound vibrations themselves, in different areas of the body, bring the healing. This chant is my remedy for the fears that arise at four A.M.

Toning, Singing Bowls, and Chant

What's toning? Simply a way to tune the body by using the voice expressively. Whether you can carry a tune or not, when you use your voice on any pitch to make a sound as you exhale, you are toning. Everyone can do it, and the effects of this natural human expression range from relieving tension and generating energy to improving concentration and stimulating the release of chemicals that positively affect the immune system. Forms of toning, chanting, or vocalizing have been used in all spiritual traditions, to clear and calm the mind before meditation or prayer, and as powerful meditations themselves. Besides having extremely beneficial effects on health, vocalizing can boost feelings of self-esteem and general well-being. One music professor who works with the voice writes, "[Because] I have watched people undergo major personality changes during their vocal studies . . . [I] have come to see that my work may be considered a healing art."[6]

Vocalizing is no less than one of the most direct ways we can affect our feelings at that mysterious point where emotions become chemicals, neopeptides and endorphins, with measurable physical properties. Because sound energy moves through matter, it may even vibrate dense areas where surgery has left masses of scar tissue, blocking the energy flow. In *The Sounds of Healing*, oncologist Mitchell L. Gaynor, M.D., advocates the benefits of sound-based therapies—chant, singing bowls, and various forms of music—to complement his cancer patients' medical procedures. What's more, he practices these therapies himself.

Tibetan singing bowls, the metal bowls of various sizes that have been used in religious ceremonies for centuries in Tibet, produce a rainbow of harmonic overtones, from low to high sounds. They are usually played by rubbing a mallet around the outside of the rim; you can learn to play one in a few minutes. The largest bowls produce sound frequencies that recall the low chanting of groups such as the

Gyuto monks from Tibet; smaller bowls have higher, more bell-like tones. The esoteric Tibetan understanding is that the bowls produce the sound of the void, a sound that Buddhist writings say, paradoxically, is full of emptiness. Resting the bowl in the palm of the hand while striking or running the mallet around the rim allows vibrations to travel through the hand and arm to the rest of the body. There are stories of bowls kept singing for hours at a time in rituals. Using singing bowls regularly also can have a profound effect on your hearing and experience of the world. You may become more sensitive to vibrating harmonic overtones in ventilation systems, refrigerators, computers, everywhere. Once you begin listening, you will hear vibration all around you.

I like to play a singing bowl as I tone to support my voice. Are you ready to begin? Relax your jaw and let your mouth drop open. As you tone each vowel *(a, e, i, o, u)* for several seconds, lightly touch your cheeks, head, throat, and chest and feel the location of vibration. Notice that the *eee* and *iii* are felt more in the head, while *ahh, ooo,* and *uuu* sounds are felt in the lower throat and chest. Make the sound that feels best at this moment and put a hand where you feel the vibration. If you're stressed from work, you'll find *ooo* is calming. But if you need a little shot of energy, try *eee*. Using vowel sounds in sexual play, by the way, can generate more excitement and also help release energy.

This singers' warm-up, which could be named "calling

in the cows," is a great way to feel different vowel vibrations. Try it in the car, garden, bed, or bath. On any pitch sing *may me ma mo moo.* Repeat it again and again, each time sliding up (or down) to the next tone of the scale as you sing *moo.* The tops of your lungs may tingle pleasantly, as if being massaged. In fact, you can think of all these practices as massages from the inside out.

When singing a vowel followed by the nasal *ng* you may hear *harmonics,* the secondary pitches that also sound when a tone is sung or struck. In fact, the voice creates a spectrum of audible and inaudible harmonics as it tones the five vowels. This is what makes reproducing the human voice so challenging for music and sound engineers. Most of us discover harmonics more or less by accident, but you may want to achieve more predictable results. Again, the shower or the car are ideal practice rooms. Close your eyes and draw in a big breath. This requires a lot of air. Keeping the lips pursed, as if drinking through a straw, release the breath in sound, keeping the jaw relaxed and open as you slowly change the shape of your mouth on the *inside* only, forming first an *ooo* sound, then an *e,* and finally a *u.* In the transitions between these vowels you can clearly hear harmonics. With patience and practice, and perhaps the help of a teacher, you can learn to amplify the harmonics until they make a colorful dance above the *fundamental* sound, that is, the pitch you're singing. The Gyuto monks from Tibet, the Tuva throat singers from Siberia, and musicians like Jill Purce are among those who have renewed people's interest in singing harmonics. Creating multiple tones in one note not only extends the capacity and range of the voice but is a metaphor for the One in Many. For some people this is a spiritual experience, like hearing *the music of the spheres*, the combined harmonies of all the heavenly bodies, which the ancients aspired to hear.

Egyptian and Greek as well as Buddhist, Christian, and Jewish hymns to the gods were based on vowel sounds. It was with the seven vowels that the Jews sought to express the God-which-cannot-be-named, though the names were commonly reduced to four sounds, each with its own power and significance. Sufi master and musician Hazrat Inayat Khan writes of the ancient practice of singing one note for half an hour to open up all the centers of the body, to create enthusiasm and energy, and to heal. As many mystics know, the effect of such repetition is to clear the mind of its usual noise, thus making space for an expanded state of consciousness. Find one tone and vowel you especially enjoy making and hearing. Tone it again and again, putting yourself in the center of the sound, and enjoy the succession of perfectly embodied moments you are creating.

The continued use of Gregorian chant through the centuries and its amazing resurgence in our time is an indication that it fulfills a need for both chanters and listeners.[7] Isn't this due to the essentially devotional intent of chant as meditation or prayer? The long phrases are without meter, following instead the natural rhythms of speech and breath. Besides its therapeutic effect on each individual, chant has a harmonizing influence on the entire community. So central was chant to Hildegard of Bingen's convent that when the Pope wanted to punish her, he forbade the nuns to chant their services. In his book *Harmonies of Heaven and Earth*, music scholar Joscelyn Godwin tells the fascinating story of a Trappist abbey in France. When chanting the Offices was limited following Vatican II, all sorts of physical illnesses and psychological disturbances—from loss of sleep to dissension among the brothers—began to occur. After the doctor who was called in, hearing specialist Alfred Tomatis, recommended resuming the chanting as before, the monks were once again able to sleep and their other complaints disappeared as well.

The chants composed by Hildegard have ecstatic passages that may include leaps of an octave (eight notes) or more. But in general the interval skips between notes in chants are small, two or three notes, which keeps the line moving smoothly. You can hear the gentle movement this creates in pieces like "Ave Generosa."* In contrast to the speed of contemporary life, the measured, simple beauty of Gregorian chant has a tranquil sensibility. One can hear silence behind and between the notes. The long exhalations required by chant empty the mind of distracting or negative thoughts and encourage physical alertness and balance. Chant can be a way of changing your own reality, which is the essence of any healing practice. Let's look now at what can happen when a group of people tone, chant, or sing together.

Strike the Harp or Join the Chorus

Why—do they shut me out of Heaven?
Did I sing—too loud?

EMILY DICKINSON

Not long ago, I sat in on a rehearsal of a chorus preparing to perform Mozart's *Requiem* at Stanford University. I watched the students straggle into the rehearsal room looking stressed and strung out. As I observed them slouched in their seats, I began to wonder why they were there at all, with deadlines looming for final papers and exams. But during the preparatory warm-ups, I noticed one, then others, begin to revive. Like dry plants being watered, they were perking up. Postures changed, eyes and complexions brightened, and by degrees the energy in the room began to rise. By the time they sang the "Dies irae," there was commitment and excitement in the air, and I realized I was among some fine musicians. They were taking this time because the music and the act of singing raised their spirits. I thought of the words of philosopher of religion Huston Smith, who said that to be happy we need a devotion to something greater than the personal self, which is "too small an object for perpetual enthusiasm."

Who would not want to be lifted like this by music? From carefully auditioned choirs to come-one-come-all choruses, there is a place for everyone. And those who sing or chant together know that nothing builds community better than mingling voices in the same vibrational field. Singing creates bonds of solidarity that are able to tolerate differences. You don't have to, you may not want to, know one another's stories in order to feel mutual support and kinship.

If you can't find a group to join, you can organize your own circle. A few people singing together make a great natural organ. It's easy to facilitate a group toning (the second Music Break tells how). Writers speak of finding their creative voices, but we all need to find and liberate our voices from self-imposed or cultural restraints.

Music, like most everything else, begins at home, with lullabies, hymns, and folk songs. Children love the song from the movie *Johnny Appleseed,* which was our little girl's favorite way to say grace. "Oh, the Lord is good to me and so I thank the Lord, for giving me the food I need, the sun and the rain and the appleseed. The Lord is good to me." For young children, there is a song for everything: "Clean, clean, jellybean" for bathing, "One, two, buckle my shoe" for getting dressed, "I wanna ride in the car-car" for driving. Everything's more fun when it's rhythmic. That's the secret of rap music's popularity with the young.

It's a natural consequence of loving music to want to make it ourselves. Who hasn't sung along with the radio or stereo? The good news is that it's never too late to begin— or begin again. More and more adults are taking up music late in life. You don't need to wait until you're struck with a life-threatening illness before pursuing your dream of singing torch songs, playing Bach or the blues, strumming a banjo, or beating a drum. But, remember, your desire to play must be greater than your fear of embarrassment or failure. You may need to remind yourself, repeatedly, that you're just doing this for yourself, and that comparisons with others are odious.

Take time and care in choosing a teacher. A good teacher may mean the difference between success or failure, and by success I'm referring not only to what you learn but to how much you enjoy the process. In *Doctor Faustus,* a novel full of fascinating musical insights, Thomas Mann says the teacher is "the personified conscience of the pupil." When you do find one whose judgment you trust, who stimulates your musical thinking and makes suggestions kindly, "grapple him [or her] to thy soul with hoops of steel," in the words of Shakespeare's Polonius!

Because music has so many components—emotional, spiritual, and physical—patience is needed on all sides. All but the most gifted (or inflated) beginner need large doses of positive reinforcement along the way. Good musicianship means cultivating an ear that is always imagining and asking for a more beautiful or more expressive sound. The better you learn to hear, the more you'll ask of yourself, and that's half the fun of it: another goal is always in sight. Gabriel Fauré, the composer of so much voluptuous music, said, "For me art and music consist of raising ourselves as high as possible above that which is." A huge order, yes, but it's thrilling to try.

As for practicing, rather than using discipline as a weapon against ourselves, think of it as an outgrowth of your desire to spend a little time every day with what you love. When desire is joined to discipline, miracles are possible. A student who had studied only a few weeks once brought me to tears with her playing of a simple piece from Schumann's *Album for the Young*. Edgar Degas, an artist who understood repetition to be the essence of craft and beauty, was intrigued with the relationship between repetition and mastery. It was precisely the ritualized, often unglamorous, movements of the ballet dancers he observed by the hour before beginning to paint, that interested him. Realizing in advance that learning a skill involves a certain level of tedium makes it easier to accept the process. Athletes know this, just as musicians do.

When valleys of discouragement and boredom appear, a teacher can help you rise above them. Most teachers appreciate and solicit feedback about what you like to play, or don't. One solution to keeping music fresh while it gets "into the fingers" (as pianists say) is to keep several pieces going at once. This is what Victor Margolis proposes in his book *The Plate Spinner*. Both plate spinning and juggling are good metaphors for keeping several pieces of music in the air simultaneously. The long-term goal of plate spinning is to be able to play several different pieces well; the short-term goal is to remain sensitive to the special sounds in each one. You need the spice of variety so that you can play music every day that suits your moods, hormones, or simply the weather. Although this method may not be for everyone, it also offers the advantage of learning a small repertoire of music over time, rather than overworking one piece until it's learned before beginning another. Music learned gradually seems to go deeper and be retained longer. And each time you return to an "old" piece, your muscles are more relaxed and you come closer to *playing*, not *working*, your instrument. If you're lucky, and willing to be a bit compulsive, a particular piece may draw you on like the songs of the sirens in *The Odyssey*.

In *Walden*, when Thoreau writes, "The mass of men lead lives of quiet desperation," he might have added, "and go to their graves with their song still in them." What are you learning besides a skill when you sing or play an instrument? A way of uniting touch, breath, mind, and heart. A way of unifying the whole self. The way each person touches the piano keys or shapes a musical phrase is unique and determines the quality of the sound produced. Because touch and phrasing communicate intention, even the playing of technical masters may leave us cold and unmoved if it doesn't come from the heart. An amateur, that is, a *lover*, sometimes communicates more. So go ahead, make a joyful noise! It's never too late to flap your wings, sing your song, and be a fool (for love) again.

MUSIC BREAKS

Finding Your Own Song

Sit or lie down with your eyes closed. Review the day's events, personalities, and situations, with an awareness of any lingering regret, anger, or frustration you may carry. Hum, or tone a vowel sound, whichever feels most healing, into the place your emotion feels concentrated and continue until the emotion begins to dissipate. There is a deep intelligence in the body that knows what it needs, if you take time to listen.

Tuning a Group

First, loosen up by moving or dancing around the room to a rhythmic piece of music, beating drums, or playing handheld instruments. A lively dance piece from the Kronos Quartet's *Pieces of Africa* will usually get everyone on their feet. When the group is ready, lie down with heads forming the center of a circle. Instruct group members to let sounds arise when and as they wish. Keeping the eyes closed will help you enter a world where there are no wrong sounds, only voices of different colors. Be silent at times and listen to what others are doing before adding your sound again to the whole. Try different pitches, high and low, and soft and loud dynamics. Don't let your sounds become too complicated or it will be difficult to hear the sound structure you're all creating together. Dissonant or clashing sounds may develop and change the mood and color. When the time is right, let sound die out naturally and rest in the fullness of the silence that follows.

SIX

The Alchemy of Music

The music that ushered in the cosmos plays on,
inside us and around us.

BRIAN SWIMME

O ur habitual thoughts eventually create an energy field powerful enough for others to detect. With music we can alter this field. Different sound vibrations stimulate new patterns of thought and behavior. Many of us experience this every day, listening to music on the car radio on the way to work to "rev up" and, after work, to relax and shift away from the concerns of the day. Music reminds us that, at least potentially, we are complete and have everything we need to be happy—something we may forget in the stress or speed of the moment.

We've seen how music can be a container for the trans-formation of musical materials. Now we'll explore it as an agent of transformation for the listener and suggest specific ways of using music to balance the emotions, restore equilibrium, and positively affect our well-being. There is plenty of evidence to confirm what our intuition may have already known—forces that change your mood and outlook, as music does, may influence health. A recent study reported that a group listening to Pachelbel's Canon showed a greater increase in positive immune response than the groups using imagery and other stimulation.[1] But it seems that the more you know, the more responsibility you must take for choosing your psychic and emotional diet. If in sickness the body is *out* of harmony, what is it to be *in* harmony? And what can you do to promote this state?

Today's alternative or complementary healing practices try to integrate ancient wisdom with new technologies. Arguably the greatest physician in history, the extraordinary Galen, whose ideas remained popular from the second until the end of the nineteenth century, believed that a person's temperament (from the Latin *temperare,* to *mix*) came from the mixture of warm-cool and dry-moist characteristics that in turn were related to the balance of the four humors (melancholic, phlegmatic, sanguine, choleric) and their corresponding elements (earth, water, air, and fire). This system of individual wholeness was picked up by the alchemists of the Middle Ages and Renaissance and, in our time, by psychologists such as Carl Jung, who used it as a poetic guide to integrating the whole personality. Jung shared the alchemists' belief that opposites in the soul must be identified before they can be united.

I have found Jung's model a useful guide in helping people choose music for balance and specific needs. There are fascinating parallels between the properties of the elements and psychological and musical qualities. Intrinsic to alchemical thinking, for instance, is the idea that the elements are transmutable. Water evaporates into air when subjected to the heat of fire; earth can be made into a solution when mixed with water, and so on. Similarly, when you learn to take your emotional and spiritual pulse, you can, if you desire, bring about changes in the elemental mix of your own chemistry. Though temperament may be inherently biological, it is also susceptible to external events—such things as climate, diet, and the stimulation of arts like music. You can begin by identifying the element(s) with which you feel least comfortable or related. Often this one will be most useful to you in attaining and maintaining your equilibrium. If you can then identify the element that is dominant in your nature—earth, water, air, fire—you will have some tools to temper extremes of mood and behavior.

Presently we'll see how music comes into this process. But bear in mind that large musical works are too complex for neat boxes. Most music of any length includes all the elements—whole fistfuls of emotional affects. One measure of a great work that has stood the test of time is its completeness. This introduction is meant as a guide to thinking about music in new ways and as encouragement for practicing your own musical alchemy. More selected music for each element is listed in "Sound Journeys" at the back of the book.

Earth

Music of the earth is full of feeling, and your physical body is a vessel for the entire range of emotions. When earth music is "moist" and warm, it evokes an immediate emotional response and may revive memories of love and passion that have a strong emotional charge. Stringed instruments, low voices (bass, baritone, and alto), and instruments that draw energy up from the depths are especially conducive to warming the heart. The passionate, highly personal expression of Romantic composers Schumann, Chopin, and Liszt stirs up earth energy, as do the cello concerti of Dvořák and Elgar and the violin concerti of Beethoven and Bruch. Brahms, whose mass, *A German Requiem*, celebrates the earth, composed beautiful works for lower voices—the *Alto Rhapsody*, the cello sonatas, and *Two Songs* (Opus 91) for viola and mezzo soprano. Rustic folk dances carry earth energy in the music of Bartók and Stravinsky. Beethoven's Symphony No. 6 (Pastorale) goes through various moods inspired by the countryside, from the happy feelings aroused on arrival to the fears aroused by a thunderstorm and the joy of its conclusion. Vaughan Williams's Symphony No. 3 (Pastoral) and Vivaldi's *The Seasons* stimulate nature imagery. Sibelius, in *Finlandia* and the symphonies, is another master painter of nature. Mahler expresses both his love of the earth and a recognition of its sorrows in *Kindertotenlieder*, but his consummate earth music is *Das Lied von der Erde* (The Song of the Earth). Here, in setting Chinese poems to music, Mahler searches for the eternal dimension in life and death and tries to reconcile human sorrows with the joys of nature and the warmth of intimacy.

Jazz, blues, and music with strong rhythms are a connection with earth energy. In the rituals and religious observances of many cultures the drum is the essential, earth-grounding instrument, able to rouse the body's natural rhythms. Sometimes called the heartbeat of the earth or Great Mother, the drum has long been used by shamans to produce trance states for healing purposes.[2] In music for drums, folk dances, Cajun music, flamenco dances, and the tangos of Astor Piazzola, you can feel the energy of the earth through your feet and legs.

Grounding in the emotional body can be essential for those inclined to abstraction. If you're feeling rigid or dry, for example, and want to feel more emotionally alive, you might put on Rachmaninoff's Piano Concerto No. 2—gorgeous and sensual, with stormy passages alternating with movements full of longing. On the other hand, if you're feeling weighted down by earth, you can shift your focus with airy music that sets you free to dream, such as Debussy's *Prelude to the Afternoon of a Faun* or his delicious "Dr. Gradus ad Parnassum"* from *Children's Corner*, Vaughan Williams's *The Lark Ascending*, Mendelssohn's Overture to *The Hebrides*.

Water

Water is associated with the less conscious parts of the soul, which are glimpsed in dreams and through visceral reactions to the visual arts, dance, and music. Sexuality is associated with water (unless it has the heat of fire). The water element of your temperament moves in circles: it can be introspective and moody, prone to reverie, brooding, and sometimes melancholy. To the alchemists, water symbolized the original amniotic fluid to which one returned for rebirth, as in Botticelli's famous image of Venus, the goddess of love, being born from the sea. Water is also the home of the Greek god Dionysus, associated with wine, ecstasy, and fertility.

There are times when everyone benefits from the ability of water music to soothe and cool the spirit. After a hectic day at work, you may need the refreshing emotional shower of music like the Schumann *Arabesque* before you're ready for dinner or the company of friends. And if the day has left you feeling arid and dry, you can use water music as a healing lubricant. Vivaldi's music for guitar and mandolin is as refreshing as the sound of mountain water. So is Debussy's "Dr. Gradus ad Parnassum."* In his *L'Isle Joyeuse*, inspired by Watteau's painting of the pleasure island of Cythera, the rocking waves suggest sensuous revels. These and other water pieces by Debussy, Fauré, and Ravel can lead to stimulating reveries. At stressful times, music with water running through it softens your edges and dissolves tension, making you feel more fluid, and perhaps more sexy.

When you're feeling emotionally arid or earthbound, try listening to Schubert's popular "Trout" String Quintet and the Impromptu No. 3* and No. 4 (Opus 90); they ripple with purling streams, cascades, and waterfalls. Smetana's powerful evocation of a river, *The Moldau,* is another good choice. In alchemical terms, a substance must be dissolved before it can be re-formed in a different configuration. This means that if you feel some hardness of the heart you may need to shed tears before feeling can melt and soften. Harp music like Mozart's Concerto for Flute and Harp or Händel's Harp Concerto, Opus 4, No. 6, brings the refreshment of an emotional shower. Music that catalyzes strong emotional responses of any kind—gratitude, grief, or joy—makes it easier to let go of a fixed attitude and see things from a different perspective.

Self-absorption and emotional instability may mean too much water in the temperament. This can be countered with music that has fire and air—a mythic dimension to ground your ego in a greater reality. The grand scale of Baroque music places you within the bigger picture—Bach's organ toccatas, Handel's *Royal Fireworks Music,* or Ravel's *Daphnis and Chloé.* The music of Vangelis, such as the soundtrack from the film *Chariots of Fire,* is a connection with the mythic dimension of the imagination. After all, we are the stuff of stars; the elements that make up the body literally fell from the sky.

Air

Air is associated with spirit, inspiration, intuition, and breath. *Wild air, world-mothering air,* wrote poet Gerard Manley Hopkins. Air represents both the intellect, with its interest in meaning and pattern, and the intuitive, insightful side of the temperament, which is prone to fantasy. In alchemical language, sublimation refers to what happens when a heated substance becomes a gas or vapor. In practical terms, sublimation refers to the way you may direct the energy of an emotion or impulse into a culturally higher activity—diverting sexual energy into work or art, for example. If the imagery associated with air and upward movement—ladders, towers, stairs, flying—is appealing to you, air energy may be a strong influence.

The spirit is free to roam, imaginatively, anywhere, which may be desirable if you have been too earthbound.

Wagner's Prelude to Act I of *Lohengrin* and Vaughan Williams's *The Lark Ascending* are tranquil and yet triumphantly soaring. Mozart's Clarinet Concerto (K. 622), a faster movement from one of his piano concerti, or Debussy's "The Maiden with Flaxen Hair"* can lighten a heavy heart. Ravel's "Pavane for a Dead Princess" is otherworldly and uplifting. The blind composer Rodrigo wanted his *Aranjuez Concerto* to sound like "the unseen breeze ruffling the treetops," and it does. Pieces played with the breath allow you to hear air producing sound. Wind instruments such as the clarinet, flute, oboe, and Japanese bamboo flute (shakuhachi) can create a sublime atmosphere. Bach's Sonata for Flute and Harpsichord in B minor, No. 1 and Mozart's gorgeous Serenade for Winds, K. 361, which may have been used at his wedding, are good choices. Music that carries you above the earth to a transcendent realm, like Fauré's "In Paradisum"* from the *Requiem*—are healing at times of loss, illness, and death. If you like New Age music, its spacious texture can help you enter dreamlike inner spaces.

When feeling excessively airy, in danger of rising like a balloon, you can ground yourself by listening to ten minutes a day of drumming, earth music, or better still, by playing your own drum. Or try walking—if possible, with your feet on the earth rather than on pavement—with one of Brahms's symphonies or his *Alto Rhapsody* in your Walkman.

Fire

Fire is the transformative element that heats things up, for chemists and cooks, psychologists and musicians, and artists of all kinds. Like the earth, we are fire at the center, dependent on the electrical charges of firing neurons to trigger the workings of our brain, heart, and nervous system. The gift of the fire of creativity, inspiration, and passion are at the core of our emotions, actions, and motivations. Is it any wonder that fire has always been associated with the realm of the gods? It's through the fire of love, when selfishness burns away, that relationships are purified. Fire needs fuel, and passion is the heart's fuel. In the words of Sufi writer Llewellyn Vaughan-Lee, "Love is the fire and we are wood." To understand the quality of a love, ask what that love serves. Each element contains its opposite, and fire can be destructive as well as purifying. It gives off sparks and can make us impulsive and quick to act and react. Think of the heat of unchecked anger and of lust or jealousy.

To bring an alchemical understanding to tending the flame of your life means being conscious about when to increase or decrease the heat of the dynamic passions. Water can put out a fire that has become too hot or begun to rage out of control. The alchemists recognized that fire must be controlled and confined to a hearth. Music can be your hearth, where the heat of passion and conflict can burn safely. Musically, the spirit of fire is conveyed by intense expression, exciting rhythms, accelerating tempos, and dynamics that build to a pitch. Beethoven increases the heat to conclude all his symphonies, and the ending of the Ninth is particularly ecstatic. There is fire in Bach's toccatas and in Wagner's overtures to *Flying Dutchman, Meistersinger,* and *Tannhäuser,* and smoldering erotic fire in his *Tristan and Isolde.* The Gypsy-influenced music that runs through Liszt's Hungarian Rhapsodies and Brahms's Hungarian Dances is igniting. Or you might listen to the fiery last movement of Brahms's Violin Concerto, portions of Schumann's *Kreisleriana,* Chopin's Polonaise in A flat (Opus 53), Manuel de Falla's *Ritual Fire Dance,* Khachaturian's *Sabre Dance,* or Stravinsky's *Firebird* and *Rite of Spring.*

Now, with all four elements in mind, if you were to choose three adjectives to describe your state of mind, what would they be? Do you have one ruling mood or passion? Do you feel restless, agitated, calm, bright, dull, heavy, dreamy? If you feel the dominance of one element, what music might express it? And what music might enhance, balance, or transform it? If you're feeling cold and detached, for example, you might warm your heart with passionate French love songs, romantic Spanish guitar music, or the hotter movements of Brahms's Violin Concerto.

In a musically attuned life, you would honor all four elements as different aspects of your soul seeking expression. This was the approach used by Marcilio Ficino, the great Renaissance philosopher, who practiced his imaginative therapies for emotional balance on leaders such as Cosimo de' Medici. Using methods that are still widespread today, from playing instruments to taking long walks and handling precious stones, Ficino treated lethargy and pessimism with particular instrumental timbres and modes. The scholars, who tended to think in concrete academic terms, for example, were urged to play stringed instruments, for their qualities of soulfulness, and to dress in white clothes rather than black, to lighten up and prevent excessive melancholy.[3]

Composing Your Life

Greatness of soul is not so much mounting high and
pressing forward, as knowing how to put oneself
in order and circumscribe oneself.
—MONTAIGNE, "ON EXPERIENCE"

You can, in most circumstances, even amid the daily pressures which inevitably pull you out of shape, maintain equilibrium and health if you think it's important to do so. Our bodies are energy systems, and as an energy mover, music can reinforce any quality of energy you desire. But you must be clear about your intention. *Entrainment* accounts for why music with a certain rhythm or mood is contagious and can change your mood. For according to the law of entrainment, if two rhythms are being played in a room, the more powerful one will draw the other into resonance with it. Entrainment occurs because nature tends toward harmony. A music therapist helping a client suffering from depression would begin by playing music that mirrors the client's depressed state and then *gradually* work up to music that shows the client how to access and explore other qualities. The reasoning? In a depressed mood it may make you feel even worse to hear lively music; first you need music that supports and joins you where you are. The question to ask in any kind of music therapy is, What qualities am I trying to bring to life or reinforce?

You may have your own version of this, but here is mine. If I'm feeling emotionally flat or drained at the end of the day, I might begin by putting on some music that matches my mood, maybe a soulful cut from Annie Lennox's *Medusa* or Miles Davis's *Sketches of Spain* or *Kind of Blue*. If I want something deeper, more profound, I might listen to the Lento movement from Beethoven's F major String Quartet (Opus 135). As I listen it is helpful to try to think of a word or two that describes how I'm feeling. Not just *tired* or *depressed*, but one more specific, such as *discouraged, repressed,* or *frustrated*. Next, I might try to find music I can move to, slowly at first, a bittersweet Chopin mazurka or a stately Greek dance from the soundtrack of *Mighty Aphrodite*. Letting the music move me, literally, is the surest way I have found to let go of burdensome thoughts and feelings. As I move I begin to feel lighter and freer—I forget myself in the pleasure of moving. And often, happiness sneaks up on me from behind. It seems that once an emotional mood has been fully expressed in music, it's easier to wipe clear the day's slate and go on to something new.

Folk music in particular takes into account the dual nature of the soul, its sadness, its joy, and the fine line between. Yiddish klezmer, like Gypsy music, often begins slowly with whatever complaints are weighing down the spirit, then gradually builds to a frenzy. You can hear this in selections on Itzhak Perlman's CD *In the Fiddler's House*. There have always been those who knew instinctively how to use music for ecstatic release. What are rock concerts, after all, but events that promise the possibility of communal catharsis through music?

A large capacity for varieties of emotional experience is the mark of a complete person, and it's in the interest of your health to give at least imaginative or artistic expression to your complexities. According to Henry Dreher, an acknowledged expert on health and medical research, it's not the negative emotions themselves but our failure to *express* them that can be injurious.

Research has shown that our health is protected when we express the full range of emotions, including the so-called negative ones. When we find constructive ways to express anger, grief, and fear, we prevent lapses into hopelessness, depressions, and passivity. . . . Unless we explore and express these primary human emotions, we cannot receive the information they carry.[4]

Dreher's views are echoed by Roger Dafter, the associate director of the Mind-Body Medicine Group at UCLA. In a recent interview, Dafter said we should embrace the full spectrum of our emotions, calling them "an innate pharmacy" in which each plays its part in healing and each is a teacher. The faster our lives, the more data we process daily, and the more numbed to feeling we may become. Music helps us break through the heart's protective armor and brings us back to our senses so that we can decipher, safely, the information carried by our emotions, especially those we may deny or repress.

I'm not recommending that everyone suffering from depression should dance two tangos and call me in the morning. Still, there are times when musical prescriptions are very effective—and, I can assure you, there are no negative side effects! Behind the ubiquitous medieval apothecary garden was the belief that for every illness a healing plant exists, and, I believe, for every need there is healing music—if you can find it. Gioacchino Rossini, the popular opera composer of the early nineteenth century, prescribed his own musical doses: "I take Beethoven twice a week, Haydn four times, and Mozart every day."

Whatever music brings together the fragments of our disconnected minds, our broken hearts, and our scattered spirits, is healing. Our challenge, living with the chronic stress of modern life, is to hear the music through the noise. To be balanced means coexisting in tension, like a note in a vibration—holding yourself in the good and evil, the joy and sorrow of life. This may be a greater challenge today than ever before, and it's to be expected that the goddess Harmony, the daughter of Venus (Love) and Mars (War), may at times elude us. But as the contrasting themes in a classical sonata or symphony suggest, opposites do attract, and as nature knows, they long to unite.

A Musical Day

The transformative potential of living with music chosen with conscious attention to your needs cannot be overemphasized. Below are specific musical strategies for times of the day when music can make your shift from one activity to another more graceful. They will help when you most need centering, stimulating, or calming. To take all of these suggestions in a single day would be a musical overdose—although it might be fun to try on a weekend. Start with one or two ideas that appeal to you. Local radio stations often use a similar approach, but you can program an entire musical day to your own taste, minus the commercials and traffic reports.

ON WAKING

In the morning when you are most receptive to the spiritual suggestion of music, Gregorian chant and other early music provide a gentle bridge between the night and day world. Nothing influences the way you live a day more than the images set in the body during the first few moments of consciousness. Every spiritual tradition has prayers and meditations for beginning the day with an attitude of wonder, gratitude, and reverence for life. The music of Hildegard* and Palestrina,* sacred works by Thomas Tallis (his divine "Spem in alium" sung by The Sixteen Choir version on the Chandos label is superb), and collections by early music groups will shine a warm light over your day. Look for recordings by such groups as Sequentia, the Tallis Scholars, Hesperion XX, the Anonymous 4, and the Hilliard Ensemble (whose CD *Officium,* with pieces by Morales, Dufay, and others is especially beautiful). Purcell's *Anthems* is majestic and devotional. Along with the matchless morning songs of the birds, these works can be used like a prayer with whose spirit you can align yourself.

AFTER COFFEE AND BREAKFAST

To pick up the pace and help you organize the details of the day, there's nothing like the Baroque boost of balanced, focused music by Bach, Händel, Scarlatti, or Corelli. If it's a special day, or simply one that asks to be celebrated with the ring of golden brass, listen to trumpet music by Vivaldi or Gabrieli. It can lift the most earthbound spirit to celestial heights. Slower Baroque movements, an adagio or andante paced to the rhythm of the heart, have been shown to be effective adjuncts to learning, organizing, and retaining information.[5] If you need a jump start before walking or exercising, pop a lively movement from a Vivaldi cello concerto or a Mozart piano concerto into your Walkman. And if you like Mozart, you will almost certainly like Haydn, a good-natured and witty companion at any time. Haydn practically invented the string quartet, and with eighty-three to choose among, you won't run out soon.

FOR A MID-AFTERNOON BREAK

Our evolutionary history suggests that we should follow lunch with a nap. Instead, we drink another cup of coffee or tea. But you might find the vitality of a lively Baroque beat more renewing than caffeine. One of Bach's keyboard concerti (the *Italian* Concerto is wonderful) or a movement from Vivaldi's *The Four Seasons* can make you feel alert but not wired. If you still need invigorating, put on Mendelssohn's *Italian* Symphony or Mozart's powerful Symphony No. 41 (the Jupiter). For a brief escape into fantasy, there is Mendelssohn's *A Midsummer Night's Dream* or Mozart's Clarinet Concerto, the music the narrator in *Out of Africa* sent wafting out over her plantation to celebrate the return of her lover.

FROM WORK TO HOME

This is the time for music with a slower tempo, music that lets the body know it's time to take care of itself. Spanish guitar music by Julian Bream, John Williams, or Andrés Segovia washes away the day's problems, easing the transition from work to relaxation. Bream's *Romantic Guitar* gently opens the heart, which may have become closed and defensive during the workday. The caress of a soprano voice singing Cantaloube's *Songs of the Auvergne* is beautiful and you may want to croon along. But if you have a big evening ahead and need to rev up, you can turn up the heat with flamenco music played by guitarists such as Paco Peña or Bob Weisenberg (especially his CD *American Gypsy*). And if an occasion demands even higher-octane fuel, there's always Wagner's "Ride of the Valkyries" from *Die Walküre*.

DURING AND AFTER DINNER

Good food, wine, and music are made for each other. Beautiful music that is not too loud, fast, or emotionally demanding sets the right mood for good conversation and digestion. In ancient cultures court musicians always played while the nobility dined. To set an elegant mood for a dinner party, there are string quartets by Haydn, Mozart, or

Schubert. Mozart's Concerto for Flute and Harp and Bach's sonatas for gamba and harpsichord, and for flute and harpsichord, are favorite dinner picks at our house. The timbre of flute and harp music lulls you into a more tranquil reality in which everything tastes better. The vibraharp of Milt Jackson on Modern Jazz Quartet's classic film score *No Sun in Venice* is as magical as light on water. If it's a rainy night snuggle in with something romantic like Keith Jarrett's collection of solo standards, *The Melody of the Night,* or classy renditions of standards sung by Billie Holiday, Ella Fitzgerald, or Diana Krall. For after-dinner singalongs, get out your favorite Broadway musicals, *The Sound of Music, The King and I, South Pacific, Show Boat.* If you're still going, there's the exuberant piano playing of Errol Garner or Fats Waller and the jazz violin of Stéphane Grappelli.

DANCE TILL YOU DROP

When your spirits are extra-high—or low—take an evening to dance. Enjoying the life of your body is a great way to slough off cares. Lighting candles and opening a special bottle of wine are two rituals that will help set this time apart. The music can be anything from the Grateful Dead or Led Zeppelin's Houses of the Holy to the soundtrack from *Zorba the Greek* or Chopin waltzes—whatever makes you happy. If you want to feel younger than your years, nothing returns you faster to earlier days than playing the music of those times.

BEFORE BED

To knit up sleeves unraveled by the day, turn off the lights, stretch out, and listen to a slow movement from a piano concerto or sonata by Mozart or Beethoven. Mozart's Adagio from the Serenade No. 10, "Gran Partita," is as soothing as a cool hand on the brow. The "Thanksgiving Movement" of Beethoven's String Quartet, Opus 132, or the luminous Cavatina* from the String Quartet, Opus 130, will bring the day to a close with the serenity of a benediction. In a lighter vein, David Darling's sensuous cello playing on *Eight String Religion* is like the comforting sound of *Om,* and flutist Tim Wheater's *The Yearning* has an exquisite tenderness that goes right to the heart. Beautiful music brings a sense of completion to a day—particularly one that has been disordered and difficult. If you are putting a child to bed, singing a gentle lullaby makes the occasion a tender ritual, as soothing to the singer as to the child.

SEVEN

The Healing Power of Music

*How can there be redemption and resurrection unless there
has been great sorrow? And isn't struggle and rising
the real work of our lives?*

MARY OLIVER[1]

Times of illness and loss can shake your assumptions
and challenge the positive attitudes and sense of purpose on which you've relied. To be pulled from an order
you've come to equate with happiness into an order in which
change is a central reality is bewildering and disorienting.
You may fear that you've been changed forever and wonder
if you'll ever again feel happy and content. Until new meaning can begin to take root—meaning informed by a broader
experience of life—most people need to go through a period of grief or sorrow.

Difficult life experiences are pointing us toward a larger,
truer view of the nature of living, though we may not be

ready to see it. And although it may not appear so at first, praise and grief are close kin. Praise is a way of honoring what is present; grief is honoring what has passed. It is the tax we pay on our attachments. As I write this, in the golden light of a late October day, the last leaves from a hundred-year-old chestnut tree are blowing past my window. Before this tree will grow new leaves, it must lose the old ones, and this is accomplished by strong winds. Our lives are no different.

Katherine Mansfield once wrote in a letter, "Like everything else in life, I mean all suffering . . . we have to find the gift in it. We can't afford to waste such an expenditure of feelings; we have to learn from it." Grief may lead you to discover that you love far more than you knew. But the heart heals in its own time and those who have come through it tell us that until hope rises again, the only cure for grief is in the grieving, Still, you can become aware of the attitude with which you meet pain in your life. If someone hurts your feelings, for example, you may react kindly and with patience, or with aversion and disgust. It's no different with a great loss. You need to show compassion for yourself. Speaking of his work with the ill and dying, Stephen Levine says that many of us are conditioned to try to escape suffering by hardening against it. He teaches an attitude of tenderness toward pain; rather than steeling yourself to it, you can practice keeping a softness in the abdomen. And you can learn to breathe in a way that makes room inside for the emotions you're trying to contain. Physical and mental attitudes reinforce each other.

So at what point can music help, and how? Initially, when grief is most acute you might need to allow the numbness with which the body protects itself from too much feeling. When the time comes that you're ready to begin facing your emotions, music that speaks to your heart can help you begin to release your pain. And music that reminds you of a loved one brings to the surface whatever may have been unfinished or unsaid between you. I have a friend who takes her guitar out to the hillside where her husband used to walk as a way of communing with his memory. Sometimes the sheer beauty of music you love—it could be the aria "O, mio babbino caro,"* from *Gianni Schicchi*—will release the healing tears.

Being cradled by music, such as lullabies or love songs, is comforting at any stage of grief. The Brahms Intermezzo, Opus 118, No. 2,* has a warm, passionate beauty and gentle rocking motion that brings the consolation of a lullaby. It is also comforting to sing or hum to yourself a simple tune from childhood, perhaps one learned from your grandmother. Lauren Pomerantz's CD *Tree of Life*[2] has been a source of comfort and inspiration to many and is often recommended by hospice workers. Both Pomerantz's music and voice have a purity that is at once deeply refreshing and strengthening. Music like this can transport us to a timeless space, where healing can occur in its own mysterious way.

There is an ancient Greek saying that the god sends the wound, the god is in the wound, and the god heals the wound. In the wisdom of this understanding there is no stage of the process when the god is not present. Nor is there a point at which you can be alienated or cut off. This is a reminder to keep the energy flowing around and through yourself, so that you don't become walled in by grief. The more you can stay connected to the larger stories you experience in the cycles of nature, to the everyday lives of others, and to the energies in music, the more receptive you will be to healing energies.

Anger, Catharsis, and Transformation

Anger and rage are common undercurrents of grief and depression, although you may not recognize them at first. "Why," a part of you is asking, "has this happened to me? And why aren't those around me suffering as I am?" Psychologists tell us that depression is often undischarged anger turned in on itself, a way of resisting the full breath of life.

Music is a good place for venting strong emotion because we know that a piece of music will last only so long, that it *will* come to an end. And by exaggerating emotion to the point of cathartic release, music enables you to experience strong feelings within a form, a safe container, that's not destructive to you or to others. When feeling is blocked, you might find a musical echo of your rage in Prokofiev's Second Piano Concerto, which was written at the time of the suicide of the composer's friend. Music like this can help you verbalize your anger, call it by name, and begin to dialogue with it in words, movement, or art. What is life asking of me? you must ask.

But there are other approaches that do *not* involve giving yourself over to anger. Many psychologists now share the view of the Dalai Lama that angry thoughts create a state of physiological arousal that doesn't dispel anger but in fact makes it worse. He writes about the disconnecting effect of the "afflictive" emotions, so called because they become obstacles to equanimity and compassion.[3] Anger, he believes, must be transformed by understanding into tolerance. This response—like that of Jesus' turning the other cheek—addresses *your* attitude, the only thing you *can* control. When overtaken by rage, it's as if you're looking through a clouded window. Music can throw open the window to the vastness of the sky. You see that there are blue patches among the clouds. When the time is right, listening to the numinous second movement of Beethoven's Piano Concerto No. 5 (the Emperor) can move you gradually into a space large enough that your vision begins to clear. It is an image in sound of a mystical acceptance and attunement with life. And you will find that the meditation at the end of this chapter (Music

Break 3), derived from the transformative Tibetan Buddhist practice of *tong-len,* has amazing power to penetrate the emotions blocking clear vision. But you must be sincerely ready to move out of the shadows toward the light.

It's difficult to think of a large musical composition that doesn't include conflict or darkness. This is an encouragement to place personal sorrow within a larger context, where it can be balanced by other realities. Music helps us remember the sensations of love, beauty, and tenderness. After a long period of grief, or anger, we may actually forget what expansiveness and dignity feel like in the body—until we hear the opening chords of Beethoven's Piano Trio in B-flat, Opus 97 (the Archduke). Or we may lose touch with the feelings of reverence and awe—until we hear the sublime Lento movement from Beethoven's String Quartet in F, Opus 135. Music can awaken us, sometimes with a shock of recognition, to aspects of our human nature that have become dormant.

Grief and pain can bruise the heart, yet we know that suffering is crucial to all the great stories of the human condition, Achilles, Odysseus, and Job. It seems to be the way we learn. What Job needed to know in the midst of his trials was that God was in his heart and would not let him go. Whatever our circumstances, we too want to feel blessed in our existence, and we *are* blessed by music that makes our hearts more tender. When we turn to the "In Paradisum"* of Fauré's *Requiem*, to Beethoven's *Missa Solemnis*, or Brahms's *A German Requiem*, we have testimonies by those who have suffered and come to know a grace beyond understanding. Intrinsic to the healing power of these works is the sense of personal grief, *my grief*, becoming part of the collective, *our grief*. Composer Roger Sessions makes this distinction in "The Composer and His Message":

> *Emotion is specific, individual, and conscious; music goes deeper than this, to the energies which animate our psychic lives, and out of these creates a pattern which has an existence, laws, and human significance of its own.*

When the sadness of a piece of music stays with you, it may be a signal that you need more time to grieve. And, given today's breathless pace, you are not likely to receive much encouragement to grieve beyond a few days or weeks. This makes the need for music that supports mourning all the greater. You will know healing has begun when your emotional range begins to return, and when sadness can have a place in your heart without defining you. In time the self-absorption of grief wears itself out. You discover you are still capable of love: your own sadness has enabled you to hear what Wordsworth called "the still sad music of humanity."

How Music Heals

I am in need of music that would flow
Over my fretful, feeling fingertips,
Over my bitter-tainted, trembling lips,
With melody, deep, clear, and liquid-slow.
Oh, for the healing swaying, old and low,
Of some song sung to rest the tired dead,
A song to fall like water on my head,
And over quivering limbs, dream flushed to glow!

ELIZABETH BISHOP, FROM "SONNET"

What then *is* healing music? There are many answers, since different needs and situations ask for different music. On the most obvious level, it's music that makes you feel better. It could be music that helps break up negative patterns of energy so that you can move on. It could be music that brings the tranquil balm of Debussy's "The Maiden with the Flaxen Hair."* Or music that has the imploring power of prayer and rouses deep sources of strength and heroism, like the intense Chaconne from Bach's Second Partita for Violin or Beethoven's Third Symphony (the *Eroica*). The most healing music in the fundamental sense may be music that carries the eternal dimension into this moment, connecting you with the larger meanings you live by. In Joseph Campbell's words,

"Eternity is not a long time, or a past or future time, but a dimension of now."

Whatever your musical preferences have been, when you're in need of emotional or physical healing, it's usually good to choose music that's less complex, more comforting than demanding, with a texture of clarity and beauty. Music that produces a relaxed state creates a climate in which healing can occur on the cellular level. Debussy's *Prelude to the Afternoon of a Faun,* Ravel's "Pavane for a Dead Princess," or the Adagietto from Mahler's Fifth Symphony are conducive to this; so are other selections listed in Sound Journeys under Music for Paradise, Mystery, and Transcendence. Slow movements from Mozart's works—the Piano Concerto in C major, No. 21, K. 467 (Elvira Madigan) and No. 23 in A major, K. 488—can help stabilize your pulse rate. Composers have instinctively recognized the regulating effect of a steady tempo on the body. As I've said, our internal rhythms, including our heart rate and the speed of our brain waves, are responsive to external rhythms. And a relaxed tempo is as infectious as a lively one.

As beautiful as Mozart's slow movements are—and beauty itself is a kind of truth—there are times when you need music that resonates with your questions and doubts, even your despair. For this you also may turn to Mozart, to the first movement of the starkly dramatic Piano Sonata in A minor, K. 310, with its chromatic scales and unusual level of dissonance. The first time Mozart performed the work in public he was met with silence. The second movement is heartbreakingly beautiful. It may reflect the disturbing time around his mother's death, when she was sharing his disheartening experiences in France. We're cautioned not to make such equations between Mozart's history and his music, for he was a professional who could write joyful or tragic music on command. Still, it is tempting to relate what we hear, especially in his late works, with his inner state. Musicologist Alfred Einstein compares the profound Adagio movement of the G minor Quintet, K. 516, to the scene in the Garden of Gethsemane, "the prayer of a lonely one surrounded on all sides by the walls of a deep chasm."[4] A man I know almost miraculously regained his passion for living when this numinous quintet helped him release a long-held grief that had been freezing his ability to feel deeply.

Loss is such a natural and inevitable part of life, yet we're given little help in coping with it. Imagine how it might be to live with as much trust in the sorrowful as in the joyful aspects of living? The poet Rilke tells the young poet who has written him seeking advice to endure times of sadness with hope because "they are the moments when something new has entered into us, something unknown . . ."[5] He explains the source of his understanding—and Mozart's:

Do not believe that he who seeks to comfort you lives untroubled among the simple and quiet words that sometimes do you good.

His life has much difficulty and sadness. . . . Were it otherwise he would never have been able to find those words.[6]

Teenagers—and they are not alone in this—are often drawn to the music of Tchaikovsky, especially the powerful Symphony No. 6 (Pathétique); it echoes their mood swings, from gloom to soaring grandeur. Others gravitate toward the struggle for faith reflected in Brahms's First Piano Concerto in D minor. The effect of finding in music an outer expression of an inner state is like that of finding an empathic friend to whom you can confide. When asked why he often plays a sad piece when away from home, like the Sarabande from the Bach Unaccompanied Cello Suite, No. 4, Yo-Yo Ma said that Bach's expression of sorrow makes him feel less alone.

Beethoven and Mahler each met difficulty in his own way, sometimes with heaven-storming music that challenged what fate had brought: deafness and isolation in Beethoven's case, heart disease and the death of his small daughter in Mahler's. Beethoven's life and music have become synonymous with courage and triumph in the face of adversity. The great conductor Bruno Walter identified the characteristic pattern of Beethoven's music as beginning in darkness and proceeding to light. In the "Arioso dolente" of his penultimate piano sonata, No. 31 (Opus 110), Beethoven shows us what it means to go *through* grief. The halting rhythms of the two-note phrases that break off in the middle and are followed by short gasps are as close to sobs as music can be. Listening to this entire sonata is a journey through beauty to grief and, finally, exultant joy. The greater the art, as legendary teacher Nadia Boulanger said, the larger the emotions it can hold. A woman I know who survived pancreatic cancer said that after trying everything else, she turned to Beethoven's last string quartets for consolation. Finally, with this music, she was led to an acceptance and understanding that were necessary to her healing. In addition to inner healing, it happened that her cancer went into remission and she now works in a hospital as a music therapist.

It is paradoxical that at times when loss leaves us feeling most uniquely alone, we may be closest to the experience of others. Mahler's first three symphonies reach their moving conclusions only after tremendous struggle, spiritually and musically. Alternating between major and minor keys, his music seems to be asking, Is life tragic or triumphant? In his Second Symphony (the Resurrection), after the shocking climax of the scherzo there is a call for light in the alto solo, "Primal Light," which is answered with the transcendent experience of actually entering the light in the finale, "Rise up." Similarly, in the Third Symphony we can follow Mahler's path from loss to a rediscovery of meaning, beginning with seemingly irreconcilable forces that finally arrive at an affirmation of purpose and joy at the heart of life. Neither Beethoven nor Mahler was spared by grief or loss, nor were they destroyed by it.

In the generation that followed Beethoven—including Berlioz, Brahms, Chopin, Liszt, Schumann, and Wagner—we can hear all the varieties of musical expression that characterize the Romantic period. Chopin, who left his native Poland to live in Paris, composed primarily small forms for the piano—waltzes, preludes, etudes, scherzos, and mazurkas. Whatever he touched was brilliant, original, and often singable. Some of his melodies are beautiful arias, such as the theme in "Fantasie-Impromptu," Opus 66, which was set to the words "I'm Always Chasing Rainbows" in a film. The mazurkas, stylized dances in triple meter, embrace fragments of waltzes, military motives, and nostalgic references to the Polish spirit for liberation. In their interplay of stability and flux, the mazurkas reflect Chopin's conflicts and uncertainties. It is the importance given to the composer's personal emotions—together with the cult of the virtuoso performer—that distinguishes Romantic from Classic music. One biographer said about Chopin, "His heart is sad but his mind is gay." George Sand, with whom he lived for several years, described him as an angel, but with this reservation: ". . . his kindness, tenderness, and patience worry me, for I get the idea that his whole being is too delicate, too exquisite and perfect for this coarse and heavy earthly life."

All four of Chopin's piano sonatas are in minor keys, as are over half of his more than fifty mazurkas. By contrast, only two of Mozart's piano sonatas and two of his thirty-plus piano concertos are in minor keys. Chopin highlights the tension between the brighter major and darker minor in the mazurka in C-sharp minor, Opus 63, No. 3.* Listen to how it begins and ends with a hesitant figure in a minor key before moving to a more sanguine, assertive theme in the middle section. Often Chopin's melancholy passages are splashed with the military rhythms associated with his homeland—as if to rouse and encourage his spirit when it faltered or became too brooding. Perhaps this helped motivate a pianist I know to study Chopin's Fourth Ballade in F minor during her father's final illness. The hesitant opening theme is stronger with each repetition, and gradually the ballade wins its way to a gloriously extroverted conclusion. She found the music large enough to contain her experience during that difficult period. Playing the piece at his funeral was her gift to his memory.

The music of Schubert can teach us how to weave the light and the dark, the joy and sorrow, of life into a single fabric. Pianist Mitsuko Uchida says, "[Schubert] thought with his soul." I have referred to Schubert's characteristic way of breaking into a lyrical passage with a darker voice that threatens to destroy the beautiful melody, as in the Impromptu in G-flat.* But Schubert's inner dialogue is even clearer in the Piano Sonata in B-flat (Opus Posthumous), a conversation with death, in which the serene and noble opening theme is silenced again and again by the ominous rumbling of a trill in the low bass. Somehow this break in continuity only serves to enhance the beauty of the theme—

think of the single black iris in Monet's painting of the pastel garden at Giverny.

Before moving on to the use of music in the hospital, I want to emphasize the value of expressing grief through your voice, as people have always done, by wailing, keening, and crying out. Letting grief come from inside of you and out through the voice can be a tremendous relief, especially if you've been choking back strong feeling. A friend who lost her baby was helped most, she said, by allowing herself to wail along with Enya's sad songs. Singing in a chorus was the way another friend gave voice to his grief and began to find healing after his wife died.

Music for the Hospital

A world of grief and pain,
flowers bloom
even then.

ISSA

There are two means of refuge from the
miseries of life: music and cats.

ALBERT SCHWEITZER

As anyone who has visited a hospital knows, nowhere is the warmth, color, and vibrancy of music needed more than in the antiseptic environments where we go to get well. True, a certain amount of sterility is a necessary by-product of Western hygiene and good medicine. But rather than immersing patients in a setting of television blaring in every room, we could offer them the choice of good music.

In his account of hospitalization in the book *A Leg to Stand On*, neurologist Oliver Sacks recounts his remarkable personal experience with the power of music. Recovering from a broken leg suffered while running from a bull on a mountain path, Sacks had been declared medically ready to walk. But his muscles seemed to have forgotten how to propel him forward until he heard music that reminded him what motion felt like *in the body*. In his words:

> *Music . . . was a divine message and messenger of life. It was quintessentially quick—"the quickening art," as Kant called it—quickening my soul and with this my body, so that suddenly, spontaneously, I was quickened into motion, my own perceptual and kinetic melody, quickened into life by the inner life of music. . . . I was carried ahead by the ongoing musical stream.*[7]

Sacks's response echoes that of others in the healing professions who have observed the quickening power of music. Even people awakened from comas have reported following the music they heard from their hospital beds like a lifeline back to consciousness. Alzheimer's sufferers are also among

those with whom music has been used with amazing success, triggering memories of verses to songs in those who
may have forgotten everything else. I have spoken to people
confined to bed—or imprisoned—who have kept hope alive
by mentally recalling every piece of music they could.

Because pleasurable music increases the release of endorphins, the body's natural morphine, it makes us more
tolerant of pain. Many of us have experienced times when
we were too preoccupied to notice an injury. Music helps us
consciously divert our attention from pain, as well as ease it.
After a painful biking accident, the rapturous beauty of the
Andante from Mendelssohn's String Symphony No. 4, playing over and over on the car stereo, got me through a long
drive to the hospital. Acting like an opiate, the sweetness of
the music partially masked the pain.

Nothing speeds up the healing process more than connecting with preexisting inner resources and good health.
To help a sick friend or relative choose the right music at the
right time ask them, What music is most associated in your
mind with a happy, vibrant time in life? Even if your body
is not able to romp along with a Mozart allegro or a favorite
Cole Porter ballad, your mind can dance. A certain piece
might carry just the quality of energy to become your own
image of health and recovery, as it did for Sacks.

When a friend of mine who always knows instinctively
what she needs was hospitalized, she found she was singing
to herself all her favorite hymns: "Abide with Me," "Lead,

Kindly Light," "Amazing Grace," and "Swing Low, Sweet Chariot." Spirituals and hymns were meant to inspire us, to call upon the deep reserves of strength in the human spirit. The hymns we sing in childhood often stay with us. At trying times I've sat at the piano and played a few verses of "Come, Come, Ye Saints," a beautiful hymn about the hardships endured by pioneers who walked or pushed handcarts across the continent, many dying along the trail. The rousing chorus, "All is well! all is well!" unites me with those who've met life's demands with faith and courage.

When visiting a friend in the hospital, you can bring a tape of his or her favorite music, or one of yours. And a portable tape player costs no more than a flower arrangement. A Mozart piano concerto or music written for cello are always appropriate. The beautiful low register of the cello makes it effective in easing pain, as low tones are generally more soothing than high-pitched ones. For me the sound of the cello is like *Om*. A patient who is able to use art materials (such as postcard-sized watercolor paper) might like painting or drawing whatever the music brings to mind. With a little experimenting we can help one another find the music for *anything,* from the pain of the moment to the hope of future joy. When a family friend had stopped eating and grown listless after being diagnosed with a serious illness, we aroused his inner rebel, whose fighting spirit can speed recovery time, by bringing him the music from *Zorba the Greek.* It worked like a spring tonic; we could almost see his energy rise. Alchemically speaking, this music turned up the heat. After all, we are rechargeable batteries! As doctors tell us, docile patients may be easier to handle but they don't leave the hospital as soon as feisty ones.

Expression is both the way of health and the way back to it. Conductor David Blum describes how he drew comfort and strength from music during his battle with cancer when, at different stages of his treatment, he listened to music he felt would have healing power for him. Having to face radiation therapy, which brought on nightmares of entering a deep, dark cellar, he listened to Beethoven's Third Leonore Overture, written for the opera *Fidelio*. He found that by identifying with the hero of the opera, who was confined to a dungeon, he himself began to feel more brave and fearless. At another time, feeling terribly alone before surgery, he calmed himself with the serene beauty of Mozart's Clarinet Concerto, K. 622. Turning his attention to the positive spirit of this music was an expression of his love of life and helped to insulate him against his suffering.[8]

And in the final hours and days of life, music can dramatically change the quality of life for the dying, as well as for their family and friends. The Chalice of Repose Project in Missoula, Montana, has pioneered the use of palliative music from voices and harps, with musicians trained to work with the dying. Founder-musician Therese Schroeder-Sheker was inspired by the practices of the Cluny monks in twelfth-century France, who would hold, sing to, and play for dying brothers.[9] Could the soul have a more harmonious passage from life to death?

Hearing is the first sense to develop in the womb. As Dr. Alfred Tomatis points out in *The Conscious Ear*, the ear is fully evolved at four and a half months, but hearing may actually begin prior to that. And often hearing is the last sense to remain. Anesthetized patients have reported being able to hear conversation and music during their surgery, and those who work with the dying assure us that the kindness of words, music, and touch may be sensed even when ordinary consciousness is lost. When music is not available (or even when it is), simply humming a tone with someone—or for them, if they are too weak—brings comfort and peace. At a time of loneliness or fear, a vibrating tone is a connection between one soul and another, a bridge of sound between life and death.

MUSIC BREAKS

The God Is in the Wound

Nothing makes it easier to regard ourselves kindly, and with compassion, than music whose harmonies touch us tenderly. Write one or two sentences about how you feel at this moment; then, listen to Mozart's Adagio from the Violin Concerto, No. 3 in G major, K. 216* or Schubert's Andante from the Piano Sonata in A major, Opus 120*, offering your grief up to the music. Tears may come, and if you notice any tightness in your body, try to release it and be carried into the emotion of the music. Let yourself receive the energy of each note, changing harmony, and rhythm. Move your hands or body or vocalize with the music if you wish. When the music ends, write a few words about what you're feeling now. Has there been change?

Transforming Darkness to Light

This may be done sitting or lying down, but requires concentration. Begin playing the Adagio from Ravel's Piano Concerto in G major,* inspired, Ravel said, by Mozart's music. Turn the volume low, following the breath in and out, allowing the body to be as comfortable as possible and taking care to expel the air fully with each exhalation. Visualize the beauty and spaciousness of the music coming into you in the form of rose and gold light. Watch the light move into the area of your chest and heart and spread throughout your body. Observe the light as it grows in power and gradually meets the dark cloud of your anger or grief. Like watching the sun break through a heavy sky after a storm, observe the light grow in intensity within you until it penetrates the darkness.

Healing with Beauty

This is a transformative exercise that can change the way we regard ourselves. Choose a musical selection such as the aria "O mio babbino caro"* or the Schubert Impromptu in G-flat, Opus 90,* whichever seems more beautiful to you. Sit or lie down and close your eyes. Breathe along with the music, feeling gratitude for the pleasure it gives. Then, with your breath, take the music into the heart area, allowing its warmth to spread throughout your body. Breathe the music deeply into the area that feels injured, unacceptable, or unforgiven.

EIGHT

Dreaming and Dancing

Work of the sight is done . . .
Now do heart work
On the pictures within you.

RAINER MARIA RILKE

Dreaming by Day

When the routine of daily life dulls the dreamer in us, music can create an imaginative space for reverie. *Reverie*, to borrow Gaston Bachelard's definition, is dreaming with open eyes, as distinguished from dreaming while asleep. He argues that the daydream is the central dream, the conscious gratification of our hopes and wishes. Using music as an occasion for reverie is a different activity from the attentive kind of listening I have been describing. Yet reverie can be so engrossing, so revealing, that you might come to value some music specifically for the images it generates. Unlike those from your television or computer screen, images that arise while listening to music come from your own depths and carry important clues about what in your inner world is trying to get your attention.

Albert Camus believed that our life's task was to recover, with the help of the arts, "the two or three simple and great images which first gained access to our hearts." Having grown up in the West, my own images center around mountains, wide fields of pungent sagebrush, and brilliant night skies. What are yours? As the advertising world knows, images—especially those reinforced by music—have great power to move us, consciously and subliminally. The better you understand your affective response to various kinds of musical energy, the more consciously you can set up the imaginative space conducive to the kinds of images you wish to invite.

Music is itself an image, if you think of an image, as Ezra Pound did, as presenting "an intellectual and emotional complex in an instant of time." Though he was referring to poetry, music may call up even more simultaneous meanings. Composers, says British composer Michael Tippett, are creators of "images of the past, shapes of the future . . . images of abounding, generous, exuberant beauty."[1] To hear shape and image in music, I suggest listening to Gorecki's Third Symphony and to the works by Arvo Pärt, such as *Tabula Rasa* or *Beatus*. At times they seem to exist in space, offering the ear shimmering sound objects. Compositions by Vaughn Williams such as the Romanza from Symphony

No. 5 may also stimulate a whole train of imagery, a different itinerary of associations for each listener.

The psyche is boundlessly rich. Fed by people and places, the natural world, by art and music, not to mention various cultural symbols, our reservoir of imagery is brimming—if we take time to notice. "Imagination is more important than information," said Alfred Einstein, physicist and violinist. A deliciously vague little piece like Debussy's "The Maiden with the Flaxen Hair"* stimulates very positive images in many listeners, hinting at a youthful, carefree aspect of the psyche. This piece may carry you anywhere, from a mountain meadow to a tropical beach, and a whole story might unfold that can shed light on a situation in which you've felt stuck. But you must take the time to explore it as you would a dream. If a problem is weighing on you, take a few moments to write a sentence or two about it before the music begins; then see where the music takes it. Debussy said composers are people who live in a world of images, but are we any different? Here is what T. S. Eliot said about the individual nature of the images that crystallize in the memory:

> *Why, for all of us, out of all that we have heard, seen, felt in a lifetime, do certain images recur, charged with emotion, rather than others? The song of one bird . . . the scent of one flower . . . such memories may have symbolic value, but of what we cannot tell, for they come to represent the depths of feeling into which we cannot peer.*[2]

The memories and dreamy reflections that certain music arouses are fertile conditions for creativity—as the taste of the madeleine was for Proust. For me the theme from the middle movement of Rachmaninoff's Second Piano Concerto brings back an unrequited love I endured for a year in high school and helps me gather up lost details of my history. And the haunting classical guitar piece *Recuerdos de la Alhambra* carries the premonitions I had when first seeing my future husband. But doesn't every love affair have its music? A ballad associated with a former love may revive all the sensate memories of the affair. When my daughter's collection of CDs was stolen from her car she felt as if she'd lost half her life. For with music we can inhabit several time frames at once—the past, which music brings back; the present, where we are reacting to the memory of the past; and the future, into which our longings may propel us.

Compositions by French composers Debussy, Ravel, and Fauré evoke the kind of relaxed, sensuous images we associate with paintings of Impressionists Monet, Pissarro, Sisley, and Renoir. They often spawn dreamlike images of dancing figures and natural forms, water, trees, flowers, birds, and animals. Monet said he wanted his painting series of water lilies to be a kind of "visual armchair" for tired working men to sink into at the end of the day. This state of waking relaxation is usually associated with alpha brain waves. It seems that the effort of intentionally trying to produce alpha states may actually interfere with their occurrence, while certain art and music can produce them effortlessly. This may explain the healing experienced by a young elementary school teacher who was suffering from a degenerative eye condition. She established a routine of lying down after work each day and letting herself be soothed by Debussy's *Prelude to the Afternoon of a Faun*. After a few weeks of this, she recovered much of her sight, which she attributed to the deep relaxation this music made possible.

Depending on the music we choose, our reveries can move us gently in the direction of our hopes. But images can be elusive and dart away like fish. Anything we can do to objectify an image or a quality of feeling helps keep it alive and evolving. Translating the energy of an enchanting—or frightening—reverie into a painting, mandala, haiku, or fairy tale (as Jill Mellick suggests in *The Natural Artistry of Dreams*) helps give it a place in our personal history. Here is what Jung wrote about images around the time of the personal crisis that ensued when he broke with Freud:

> To the extent that I managed to translate the emotions into images—that is to say, to find the images which were concealed in the emotions—I was inwardly calmed and reassured.[3]

The image of a radiant woman dressed in white once appeared in my mind's eye while I listened to the "Sanctus" from Gounod's *St. Cecilia's Mass*. I was going through a difficult time and her image, joined with the music, brought me comfort and reassurance. Since then I have turned back to this particular music for support. More often music will evoke a quality of feeling rather than an image. Both were present in my case; the figure brought feelings of love, compassion, and protection, but was also powerful simply as an image. Great music, especially in live performance, can heighten feelings of reverence and awe. Bach's *St. Matthew Passion,* the B minor Mass, and the choral works and requiem masses by Haydn, Mozart, Beethoven, Berlioz, Brahms, Schubert, and Mahler have a history of catalyzing profound spiritual experiences in listeners. It is as if music creates a fertile ground for something new to arise.

Two recent works by contemporary composers that carry feminine energy for many people are Henryk Gorecki's Third Symphony (for orchestra and soprano voice) and John Tavener's *The Protecting Veil* (for solo cello and orchestra). With passages of ravishing, dark beauty, both compositions celebrate aspects of Mary, the mother of Jesus. Radio stations have reported that when Gorecki's Third Symphony is played, motorists often pull off the road to listen, and the station gets dozens of inquiries about it. Gorecki's music captures the mystery, wisdom, and compassion that we associate with Mary—or with the wisdom figure Sophia or a goddess figure. In our materialistic and aggressively visual culture the soul has a counter-need for feminine spiritual energy associated with the wisdom of the earth, of what is mysterious and hidden.

When music-induced reverie gives voice to suppressed or censored parts of the soul, great currents of creative energy can be released. Because it comes from the depths of its creators, art helps us sense our own depths. Leonard Bernstein was referring to this unconscious level of the creative process when he said, "The most important aspect of any art is that it not be made up deliberately out of one's head."[4] He was referring to the trancelike state of concentration that comes from tapping into the energy of the unconscious mind. We may not often feel we are acting from divine inspiration, as Bernstein seems to think Beethoven did. But if one purpose of a spiritual discipline is to increase the communication between the conscious and unconscious levels of our minds, music and reverie are important practices. Perhaps it is images the soul needs more than answers.

Reverie is most easily set in motion when listening to music while lying down. This is an invitation for music to cast us adrift on the sea of the imagination, as Baudelaire celebrates:

When music captivates me like the sea
I sail away,
Out to the faintest star the eye can see—
Anchors aweigh![5]

Like the paintings of Vermeer or Maxfield Parrish, great music helps us see with a visionary light. "The dream is stronger than experience," writes Gaston Bachelard. Artists are people who take their dreams seriously.

Dancing in the Dark

I can only believe in a God who knows how to dance.

FRIEDRICH NIETZSCHE

Music calls dance into being. Isn't the whole universe and every cell of our bodies dancing a fluid dance of creation and destruction, of energy becoming mass and mass becoming energy? As pulsating forms of vibrating energy, our bodies are force fields in a constant flux. We speak in musical phrases about "finding our own rhythm" and "being in harmony." We try to "get in step" and "join the dance." The act of dancing is a way of asserting that we're not someone to whom events merely happen but are active participants in life's inevitable twists and turns. Dancing keeps us flexible. It's the full-body way of making music, of saying yes to what is. In Romanian Gypsy communities it's customary to dance on the grave of a friend who has just been buried. In the Spanish flamenco tradition it's said that the best dancers always have death perched on their shoulders. And the older the dancer, the greater the victory of vitality, joy, and life in the face of gravity and mortality!

Do you remember in *Zorba the Greek*, when Zorba dances

on the sand? As you know if you've tried it, this feels awkward and clumsy. But life seldom provides us with the smooth floor of a ballroom; usually we have to dance *in the middle of the fighting,* as Rumi says. How does your body like to move? Have you a mental image of yourself dancing? If you're not sure, turn on a piece of music you love, close your eyes, and wait for an image to appear. If an improbably graceful ballerina or a macho tango dancer drifts across your mental screen, accept it as a gift from your psyche. Then, while the music is playing, borrow *one* movement or gesture from this dancer and try it out. Even if only your hands are moving, nothing is more eloquent, as flamenco dancers know. When the music is right, you will naturally find your own moves and gestures.

Even relationships are a dance. Writer George Leonard likes to demonstrate this truth by dancing out the patterns of coming together and moving apart, now face-to-face, now back-to-back. Sometimes the dance is as free and gay as a Mozart Rondo; other times it's as intense and proud as flamenco. To dance well you must be right in time with the music, not leaning back to the last minute or pressing forward to the next, but poised directly on the present step. Good dancing and living in the moment are intertwined. Dance to the music that *you* hear.

Dance, when you're broken open.
Dance if you've torn the bandage off.
Dance in the middle of the fighting.

Dance in your blood.
Dance, when you're perfectly free.

—RUMI/BARKS[6]

MUSIC BREAKS

Opening the Heart

Every sound can free memories of some kind. While listening to the aria "O mio babbino caro,"* you may remember the sweeping vistas over the rooftops of turn-of-the-century Florence in the movie *A Room with a View*—or you may remember a trip of your own, or your first love. As a rose opens to sunlight and warmth, let your heart open to the warmth in this music. Breathe it into an area of your life that needs more movement, beauty, and energy.

Waking Dreams

Listen to Debussy's "Dr. Gradus ad Parnassum,"* from his *Children's Corner Suite*. Let its wavelike motion carry you wherever you need to go. What colors, images, or patterns of movement does the music evoke for you? Now listen to Debussy's "The Maiden with the Flaxen Hair,"* and notice what images cross your mind. Which piece felt most delicious to you?

A Dance to Life

The Adagio assai from Ravel's Piano Concerto in G major* has been choreographed for both classical and modern dances. Let the dancer in you find gestures for what you feel when hearing this luminous exchange between piano and orchestra. For inspiration, you might read William Carlos Williams's great poem about dancing alone, "Dance Russe," a way of celebrating yourself, just as you are.

NINE

The Inner Garden

Which of the two powers is able to raise men to
the highest sphere, love or music? . . .
I think we may say, that while love can give us no idea of
music, music can realize the idea of love. But why separate
one from the other? The soul soars on the wings of both.

HECTOR BERLIOZ

By now you know that the music in this book and on the companion CDs has been selected for qualities of beauty, soul, and spirit. This music is like a garden. It satisfies our craving for perfection. It gives us a taste of paradise. For what is paradise if not a place where the heart's desire for love, light, and beauty are fulfilled? Now we're ready to explore the ways music cultivates our sensibility, creating a garden *inside*. Think about the qualities you attribute to paradise. Is it a literal or a metaphorical garden, or both?

Our first intimations of presence, God, a higher power,

the ground of being—or whatever we choose to name the unfathomable mystery of life—are connected as often to nature as they are to music. According to the imagery and mythology of creation stories in the Judeo-Christian and Islamic traditions, life began in a garden paradise, and the garden was the place for love. The Buddhists' Happy Land is also a garden, with jewel-like flowers and fragrant, flowing rivers that emit beautiful music. The word *paradise* has its etymological root in the Old Iranian word *pairi-daeza*, meaning "walled" or "enclosed," as Persian gardens were places set apart from the surrounding desert. Within the walled gardens of the Alhambra in Granada, Spain, the designs can be as intricate as Islamic architecture or as simple as stairways of running water. Within the boundaries of a complex Bach prelude or fugue the structure can grow from a theme simple enough to sing. Tonality—the organization of a piece around a particular key or tonal center—acts as a musical wall to keep out inappropriate harmonies; yet it can be strong enough to contain violent oppositions, changes of tempo, meter, mood, and notes that lie outside the primary key.

An ironic commentary on what we expect within the boundaries of a musical event is John Cage's piece *4′ 33″*, in which the pianist sits at the piano without playing for exactly four minutes and thirty-three seconds. Whatever sounds occur during that period of time are offered as the event for our contemplation. Cage has taken down the walls that separate the work from the rest of life, declaring it *all* the work. This is the musical equivalent of putting a fence around a wild patch of earth and declaring it a garden. As an effective theatrical piece, it gives the *frisson* of heightened awareness of the ordinary world. But if we have come expecting to hear music, we may go away disappointed at hearing only nervous coughs and titters.

The Education of the Heart

If our lives are an education in the imagination of desire and longing, music may be the most pleasurable way of studying the heart. Is there any emotion music cannot express? At some time we've all experienced the surprise of hearing music that seemed to reflect our innermost thoughts and feelings. And though longing tends to become focused in certain times, places, and people, it's crucial to realize that we can influence the direction of our desires, avoiding at least some of their fruitless detours and heartbreaking dead ends. We can choose music that guides our desire toward what is worthy of devotion. I'm not suggesting that we try to withdraw energy from longing. As William Blake said, "Energy is eternal delight." Whether earthly or heavenly, it is energy to be used and enjoyed, even when we choose to divert or sublimate it. Our task is to educate the passion of our longing rather than be used by it. We know we're ready to begin a garden, Robert Bly writes in *Iron John,* when we value cultivation more than excitement.

We have seen how music affects the quality of our energy. In chapter 3 we traced Beethoven's evolution from the extroverted heroism of his middle period, in the Third and Fifth Symphonies, to the maturing vision of his late quartets, informed by self-acceptance and reflection. Listening to the Cavatina from the String Quartet in B-flat major, Opus 130,* or the Lento of the String Quartet in F major, Opus 135, is a humanizing influence on a heart that may be wild and restless. In these late works Beethoven communicates a state of consciousness that sees more deeply into life. His vision can render us more sensitive and compassionate. Beethoven's musical "fingerprint" is an upward-rising melodic line, symbolic of his aspiration to raise himself beyond the personal, to touch heaven through his art. In the playful but concentrated Bagatelle, "Quasi allegretto,"* from Opus 126, we can hear the melodic line climb almost two octaves. Like other Bagatelles in the set—perhaps the last pieces he wrote for piano—this piece reveals Beethoven's quest for simplicity and immediacy. It's like a song he might have sung to himself.

Robert Schumann, the most literate composer of the Romantic generation, continues in the direction of late Beethoven, with music that is a revelation of the soul. At the beginning of his piano masterwork, Fantasy in C, Opus 17, he quotes a motto from Schlegel that ends with the words "the soft refrain that can be heard by one who listens alone."[1] Listening for this soft refrain brings us into participation with his vivid expression of a longing that is both confessional and declamatory. Schumann gives desire a shape and form, enabling us to see it more objectively, to walk around it, as we might a piece of sculpture. Longing, or *sehnsucht*, was a central theme in German Romantic literature. Schumann, like his friend Johannes Brahms, was drawn to fictional characters such as E.T.A. Hoffmann's music master, Kreisler, who believed that "yearning derived from a higher life [that] endures forever because it is never fulfilled." Great music is able to express the infinite nature of longing, which knows no limits and may, therefore, never be fulfilled, except at moments—by lovers, mystics, and other poets of the soul. In grasping this, we can guard against futile attempts to satisfy infinite longing with finite things.

Lasting visions of what life could be, should be—if we put aside greed and a desire for power—require effort as well as inspiration. In the language of the garden, the earth must be laboriously worked and the weeds must be pulled before the soil is fertile enough to bear good fruit. In the language of music, the strings of the musical instrument, a metaphor for the heart, must be tuned to prepare and harmonize the soul for love. In drawing us closer to the source of our emotions, music prepares us for the great task of love. This accounts for the images of men and women portrayed with their instruments throughout the history of art, in Persian miniatures, interiors from the golden age of Dutch painting, Watteau's *Fêtes galantes*, Chagall's airborne fiddlers, and Klee's gardens of love. As women sit at the keyboard or men cradle lutes or other stringed instruments, we can read in their wistful expressions all the attitudes of what it is to be human. The English metaphysical poet George Herbert speaks of himself as the instrument whose music would be improved by suffering of the heart:

> *Stretch or contract me, Thy poor debtor.*
> *This is but tuning of my breast,*
> *To make the music better.*[2]

For good reason, then, we refer to art as a *process*. Certainly the artist in each of us knows something about the tension between the control we can exercise over a created work and the uncontrollable flow of life. The order and beauty of finished works—framed and hanging on the walls of a museum, or bound and neatly stacked in a bookstore, or performed on fine instruments in a lovely concert hall—belie the messy studio or garage where the work was made, not to mention the disarray that may have existed in the artist's personal life. Underlying Beethoven's carefully crafted works were disturbing relationships with his relatives, and underneath his piano, a chamber pot and dirty dishes. Genius certainly doesn't demand this. Ravel, who dressed like a dandy, is a counter-example of elegance, both in his personal style and in his music. When you listen to the slow movement from his Piano Concerto in G major,* it shouldn't surprise you to learn that Ravel had Mozart in mind. And what he learned was not to let orchestral complications detract from the simple clarity of a beautiful theme. If Ravel can learn from Mozart the beauty of simplicity, so can we. As an artist of living, the question to ask as you craft your own life is, What emotion, what inner state, are you living from? Are you living out of fear or love? This story points to an answer.

Originally, of course, musical instruments were made only from organic materials such as shell, bone, wood, skins, and catgut. All these materials were once alive and growing, and as they are played, the life force continues to vibrate through them. But when asked where the music itself originates, the poet Rumi said that the music of the reed flute is the sound of its longing to be reunited with the reed bed from which it was cut. To play the music of the source, using the wind of God, the player must become hollow as the reed, a channel through which the longing plays. This is a paradigm for the artist within you, the one who *is* the music while the music plays. In choosing what that music will be, you are taking part in shaping your destiny.

Schumann and Brahms: Eros and the Artist

*What do they do,
the singers, tale-writers, dancers, painters, shapers, makers?
They go there with empty hands,
into the gap between.*

—URSULA K. LE GUIN,

"ARTISTS" FROM *ALWAYS COMING HOME*

In the Islamic tradition it is said that when the gods wish something to come into being, they plant the seed in one of us. And thus we find ourselves beginning to imagine making music, planting a garden, creating a painting, cooking a succulent dish, or writing a book. We have all felt ideas mysteriously arise in us, sometimes with the strength of a compulsion. In youth the desire to create may come from an excess of eros, like an overflowing cup; in later years, as energy diminishes, it may reflect a spiritual longing for completion. But creativity doesn't follow rules. In *Love's Body* Norman O. Brown defines *eros* as an instinct that moves us toward connection and union with life, as opposed to *thanatos*, the death instinct, which moves us toward separation or division. According to this definition, it is eros that energizes an artist to recapture the sounds and sights, the tastes and feelings, of a remembered or imagined paradise. Gauguin looked for paradise in the women and lush abundance of Tahiti; Monet in form-dissolving light on water and surfaces. Debussy found a paradise of sound in the shimmering quality of certain harmonies and note patterns as in "Dr. Gradus ad Parnassum";* Brahms in the sensuous low and middle voices in such pieces as the Intermezzo in A major, Opus 118, No. 2.* Schubert's characteristic long melodic line, heard in the Impromptu in G-flat major, Opus 90,* and also in sonatas and symphonies, was described by Schumann as having a "heavenly length." Is there music that holds the quality of your longing? Of your paradise?

The forces that drive creativity can be ruthless, and biographies of artists reveal the turbulence that can accompany a life of conventions broken in the service of the creative impulse. Jung wrote:

> The artist's life cannot be otherwise than full of conflicts, for two forces are at war within—on the one hand the common longing for happiness, satisfaction, and security in life and on the other a ruthless passion for creation which may go so far as to override every personal desire. . . . There are hardly any exceptions to the rule that a person must pay dearly for the divine gift of creative fire.[3]

According to one tradition, an artist who plays his or her instrument consummately well, a Paganini or Horowitz, may be imbued with demonic powers and have the faint aura of having made a Faustian bargain. This suggests a price must be paid for great artistry. One price of creativity for Beethoven, and for Brahms, was loneliness. Though their circumstances differed, neither Beethoven nor Brahms ever married or had a long-term intimacy with a woman. Both men spoke often of the loneliness of unmarried life but seemed resigned to solitude, even coming to view it as necessary to their work. Each was drawn to women who were musically gifted but engaged or married and therefore unavailable and "safe." As his letters reveal, Brahms's love for Clara Schumann was central to his life. But his desire for "the happiness of a family circle" was balanced by his yearning for independence. Many of Brahms's compositions evoke so much nostalgia, both for what he lacked personally and for the music of past masters, next to whom he felt dwarfed, that pianist Rudolf Serkin described Brahms as a "memory artist."

The intersection of three great artists, Robert and Clara Schumann and Johannes Brahms was momentous. No relationships influenced Brahms more over his lifetime than those with the Schumanns. When, as a young man of twenty, Brahms made a pilgrimage to the Schumann doorstep in Düsseldorf, he was already a fully formed artist. In the ex-

citement of their mutual appreciation and shared enthusi-
asms, the three artists would play for each other and talk late
into the night. Not long after Brahms's arrival, when the
mental illness Robert had felt overtaking him forced him to
voluntarily enter a sanitarium, Clara turned to Brahms as a
trusted friend. Despite the love she and Brahms had for each
other, soon after helping Clara adjust to Robert's absence,
Brahms left the Schumann household. Whatever seemed to
stand in the way of their living together—perhaps the image
of Robert himself—Brahms always referred to Clara as his
"good angel." "I have no secrets from you," he wrote to
her.[4]

Brahms's Intermezzi, sometimes called his love letters,
are among the most intimate and passionate musical expressions in piano literature. In music so personal, meant to be
played in a chamber rather than a large concert hall, the soul
of Brahms feels near. If we think of a symphonic work as a
public statement, with the formality of a large oil painting,
an Intermezzo such as Opus 118, No. 2* is closer to a drawing or watercolor. Composer Ned Rorem once declared *all*
music to be a love letter—the question is, to whom? It's difficult to know if some Intermezzi are love songs or lullabies,
but perhaps it doesn't matter. Love songs can be consoling
and lullabies can be passionate, if quietly so. The black boxes
found in the wreckage of airplane crashes have recorded pi-
lots singing to themselves in their last moments, in some
cases, songs or lullabies from childhood. In his Intermezzi

Brahms often seems to be comforting himself, as a mother would a child. The Intermezzo, Opus 117, No. 1, is preceded by the words: "Sleep soft, my child, now sweetly sleep / My heart is sore, to see thee weep."

Whatever the original impulse, the final created work is a gift of what is finest in the artist's imagination. In his novel *Apocalypse*, D. H. Lawrence says the desire of the artist within is for a salvation that is not just his own isolated one but one "connected to the living whole." Pessimism, when it exists, may come from a deep belief that transformation is possible but has not yet been achieved. Sometimes the energy of thwarted love is directed into a project. For Schumann, sublimation was imposed by the long resistance of Clara's father, who was so opposed to her marrying Robert that he tried to cut off all communication between the couple. It was during that difficult year of 1840, his productive "year of song," that Robert composed more than 130 songs, nearly half of his total body of work. The majestic Fantasy in C, Opus 17, for piano also dates from that period of personal upheaval. In the final movement a theme begins repeatedly, first in one voice and then another, only to break off before fulfilling itself. When at last the music reaches a climax, with both voices joined in ecstatic arpeggios in the final cadence, it is a consummation.

A quintessential personality of the Romantic era, temperamentally as well as musically, Schumann found in music a language for expressing the extreme aspects of his soul, from a wild effusiveness to a tentative inwardness. He gave a different name to each of his opposing personalities, crediting some of his compositions to the worldly, extroverted man of action he called Florestan, and others to the shy, sensitive introvert, Eusebius. Amazingly, Schumann was foreshadowing the technique of dramatizing different parts of the personality used in modern psychology. Roland Barthes described Schumann as a musician of "solitary intimacy, of the amorous and imprisoned soul that *speaks to itself*. . . ."[5] In addressing secluded, secret parts in us, Schumann gives us glimpses into depths we might not know were there. There are moments in compositions such as the *Arabesque* when the curtain seems to open and close quickly on a private moment of bliss. And fanciful, brilliant moments flash out from many of his piano works—the *Fantasy Pieces*, *Kreisleriana*, *Davidsbündler Dances*, *Carnival*, *Humoresque*, and *Morning Songs*.

What we learn from Schumann, as from Beethoven before him, is that the music itself helped bring together the diverse, even antagonistic, parts of his personality. Reconciliation was the reward of the work. The artist within us seeks a language and a form to contain what might otherwise remain hidden and unspoken in our hearts.

The Garden of Love

In the gardens of healing centers such as Epidaurus, where the ancient Greeks went for healing, there were shrines to Asklepios, son of Apollo and god of healing, as well as to Eros and Aphrodite. In the Greek mind, medicine and music were so intertwined that Apollo presided over both realms. It would seem that the Greeks were well aware that music and love both play crucial roles in healing. Who would question love's miraculous power to renew energy and stimulate a chain of responses, from euphoria to melancholy? At Epidaurus, those who came for healing were "incubated" in a dark room to sleep and await the arrival of a dream that brought healing.[6] Already a presence in the garden, love was invited into the seeker's dreams. Often love *was* the cure. One classical philosopher asserted that religions were "only splinters from the broken mirror of Aphrodite."[7]

The fenced or walled garden depicted by early authors and artists, the *hortus conclusus,* was defined by boundaries that protected what was inside. Mary, the mother of Jesus, is often shown within the safety of a rose garden—as roses and gardens came to be the very emblems of the feminine principle and of love, spiritual and physical. In the King James translation of the Song of Solomon, the association of lovemaking and the garden is clear, "Let my beloved come into his garden, and eat his pleasant fruits."

Although Eros is a god who may blind us, without love we may not really see at all. "Love," says Rumi, "is the way messengers from the Mystery tell us things." Is it possible to truly see the beauty of someone or something without loving it? Like the alchemical model, where gold comes only after the transformation of baser elements, the Sufi tradition teaches that the heart must be purified and polished to brightness if it is to mirror divine love. This may take a lifetime—or a crisis such as serious illness may do the work with astonishing speed. Beethoven was transformed by his strong attachment to his hapless nephew Karl and by his "Immortal Beloved." Inspired gardener Celia Thaxter, creator of the flowery paradise seen in Childe Hassam's paintings on the Isles of Shoals, saw the beloved in every flower into which she poured her soul.[8] For those of us who love music, a piece with which we feel attuned, that is *at one*, may become the very image of love. And what is it to love but to give something or someone our fascinated attention? The great Sufi musician and philosopher Hazrat Inayat Khan, for whom everything became a kind of music, calls music "nothing less than the picture of the Beloved."

Beauty connects us with what is timeless in music. Although the ephemeral quality of music and gardens adds poignance to their beauty, they aspire to a place outside time. This is what Yeats imagines in "Sailing to Byzantium," in which the artist sings from a golden bough, "Of what is past, or passing, or to come." In formal gardens the desire for permanence may take the form of marble statues, ornamental stones, or carefully placed rocks. In music the timeless element comes through in pieces so memorable that they transcend time and circumstance: arias such as Mozart's trio "Soave sia il vento"* from *Così fan tutte* and "Dove sono" from *The Marriage of Figaro;* Puccini's "O mio babbino caro"* from *Gianni Schicchi* and "Un bel di" from *Madame Butterfly;* "Casta Diva" and "Nessun dorma" from Bellini's *Norma.* However the surfaces and conditions of our lives have changed, music like this reminds us that our hearts are made to love. That has not changed.

"Every creation springs from a sort of psychological nirvana," writes Gaston Bachelard. Each work of music, then, is a fresh opportunity to cultivate a garden that contains more of the soul's imagined paradise. There are times when the creation may be in sharp contrast to its surroundings. Writing about Vermeer, whose paintings have become an emblem of serene beauty, Lawrence Weschler points out that they were created during the Thirty Years' War, when all of Europe was in chaos. Through his art Vermeer was constructing an atmosphere of harmony and peace lacking in the outer world—and most likely at home, with his wife and ten children.[9]

Like Vermeer, despite the outward difficulties of life, Mozart created pieces that give the heart a resting place. As we enter the enchantment of his music, we can put the world behind us. There are times to defend ourselves, but there must be times when we open all our senses and become utterly vulnerable—if we are to have a full response to great music, and if we are to be lovers in the broadest sense. Healing at a deep level, as at Epidaurus, means letting go of our ego so that something greater can possess us. And what is the gift of great music if not to allow us to participate for a time in the rapture, compassion, and immense vitality of great souls like Bach, Mozart, and Beethoven? And significant music continues to be composed. Among the contemporary works that can ignite the imagination and open the heart to the sacredness of things are: Arvo Pärt's *Berliner Mass, Tabula Rasa, Te Deum;* Einojuhani Raatavara's *Angel of Light;* John Tavener's *The Protecting Veil* and *Eternity's Sunrise;* and Henryk Gorecki's *Third Symphony.*

When music comes alive in you, when the outward sound becomes an image of the inward life, it brings a heightened state of awareness. Like a flower that blooms unseen for the sheer delight of it, you may feel a blossoming inside while listening to music in your home, in the car, on a bus or train. This is a pathway to a garden within. In the words of the Indian mystical poet Kabir:

Near your breastbone there is an open flower.
Drink the honey that is all around that flower.
Waves are coming in:

there is so much magnificence near the ocean!
Listen: Sound of big seashells! Sound of bells!
Kabir says: Friend, listen, this is what I have to say:
The Guest I love is inside me![10]

Mozart: The Divine Child

Prayer is the world in tune.
—HENRY VAUGHN

The magic carpet that carries many music lovers to a place of innocence in the soul—a place that never loses its desire for wonder and delight—is the music of Mozart. Investing each moment with meaning, without overloading the senses, his music is a refuge from the griefs and burdens of life, a garden where love can be protected and nourished.

From the age of three Mozart inspired an awe that led people to describe him as "touched by God." Much has been made of Mozart's childlike nature. Not only was he himself an embodiment of the archetypal divine child, but his music has led generations of listeners to the living child in them. It is music that leaves us deeply refreshed and delighted. Mozart's field of play was music, and the way he turns a phrase, changes a harmony, or pivots on one note into a new key can amaze even those long familiar with his music and the Classic style. According to his musical sister, Nannerl, who knew how discerning Mozart's musical judgments were, he retained a childlike nature throughout his life—in everything *except* his music. When it came to musical judgments, he had complete independence of thought.

At thirty Mozart was wise enough to know what really mattered and to communicate it musically. From early childhood, he had received expert musical instruction at home from his father Leopold, an astute teacher and musician. Amazingly, Mozart was able to work out most compositions entirely in his head, sometimes carrying a whole concerto around for days before putting it on paper, no corrections needed. Even so, Mozart continued to learn from every available source as he made his way around Europe as a child prodigy—opera from the Italians, fugues from Bach, string quartets from Haydn. Yet he remained essentially himself.

Nothing is more remarkable than Mozart's humanity. As his operas reveal, he was accepting and forgiving of human frailty. His music shows us by example that conflicts can be contained without forcing on them a dogmatic resolution. Humorous acceptance of human nature and, above all, forgiveness are the themes that dominate his operas—though he does consign Don Giovanni to the flames of hell because he refuses to repent for his misdeeds. Because Mozart delighted in creating music for different characters and situations, if he'd had his way, he'd have written more operas. Even so, arias predominate in his sonatas, concerti, and symphonies. They're the tuneful, often gorgeous, melodies we come away singing. Like the trio, "Soave sia il vento"* (May the wind blow gently) from *Così fan tutte,* so many of Mozart's songs are serene on the surface but full of irony and inner contradictions. Here, the cynical Don Alfonso, the male voice in the trio, has convinced his young male friends to test the fidelity of the two sisters they love. The men will pretend to go to war but return disguised as Albanian noblemen to woo the ladies. In this trio the two women and Don Alfonso bid good-bye to the young men.

Mozart shows us the ironies of living, that while one person is dying, another may be simply opening a window. All this and more happens in the first scene of *Don Giovanni.* From the first notes of the dramatic overture in D minor (like the ominous piano concerto in the same key), Mozart sets an anxious mood of impending doom. He obviously relished telling this tale of Don Giovanni's romantic escapades and perils. It allowed him to depict the Don's swaggering ego in one scene and in the next, the lament of one of the Don's wronged, wounded ladies. There are few passages in music that convey more sublime terror than those Mozart wrote for the final scene of the last act, when the Commendatore takes Don Giovanni to hell. If we cling to the idea that life should be simple, the multiple contrasts in Mozart's music point to a different reality. Through Don Giovanni, the man—an elemental power, the life force itself, never in love but always the cause of love in others—Mozart expresses the dark, irrational side of the Enlightenment.

Like all of us, Mozart wanted to feel happy. It's notable that only two of his piano concerti are in minor keys and only two of his piano sonatas. Although the slow movements in Mozart's works, passages like the poignant Andante of the A major Piano Concerto, No. 23 (K. 488), can bruise the heart, there is enough zest and liberating freedom in the spirited, kick-up-your-heels Rondo, Allegro, and Presto movements to balance the weltschmerz of a mature soul. Mozart's gaiety is the true kind, that knows about pain and suffering and sings all the more brightly because of it. He explains his musical associations in this way:

> *Would you like to know how I have expressed and even indicated the beating, loving heart? By two violins playing in octaves. . . . You feel the trembling—the faltering—you see how the throbbing breast begins to heave; this I have indicated by a crescendo. You hear the whispering and the sighing. . . .*[11]

Besides the musical perfection of Mozart's works, the French doctor Alfred Tomatis—known as the "Einstein of the ear" for his contributions to our understanding of the way we hear—has proposed concrete medical reasons for the amazing power of Mozart's music to harmonize, heal, and vitalize our systems.[12] Tomatis's research indicates that the primary function of the ear after birth is, through sound, to charge the neo-cortex of the brain and the entire nervous system. The membrane of the inner ear has far more cells that respond to high than to low frequencies. So Tomatis has used progressively filtered compositions by Mozart to retrain the ear to the kind of high-frequency sounds that filtered into our ears from our mother's voice while we were in the womb. High-frequency music charges and energizes the brain, he believes, and this may explain the improved performances of those who listened to Mozart before taking an intelligence test in the widely publicized study done at the University of California at Irvine.

But whatever the reasons for the perennial popularity of Mozart's music, it should not surprise us that he was not considered entirely acceptable in his day. "So *many* notes," said Emperor Leopold II after a performance of Mozart's opera *Abduction from the Seraglio*. "Exactly as many as are needed," Mozart replied. Whatever can be said about him as a man—his love of fine clothes (oh, how he longed for a certain red waistcoat to show off his new mother-of-pearl buttons!) and his propensity for scatological humor, drink, and billiards—the music says much more. Antony Hopkins explains why he places Mozart above all other composers:

> . . . *in his music I find everything that I require; passion, intensity, dramatic contrast, humour, delight, sorrow, profundity, daring and humanity all expressed with fewer notes and less effort than anyone else needed.*[13]

What else does Mozart's music cultivate? I know a psychiatrist who often plays the slow movement of the Mozart Clarinet Concerto (K. 633) after a patient. He says it clears his mind, brings him back into balance, and gives him the image of beauty he needs to meet difficulties. The clarinet's long, soaring phrases in this concerto—like those of the violin in the Adagio from the Violin Concerto No. 3 in G major,* or the woodwinds in the Serenade No. 10 "Gran Partita" (K.361)—can take us to a timeless dimension where thoughts of the past and future are dissolved. And the textures of Mozart's spacious Andante and Adagio movements are so transparent; even when the tone is melancholy, light and air seem to circulate around each note. In a moment of beauty we may drop into a more healing reality, an inner garden closer to our heart's desires. Isn't it from this place of connection with our soul that we long to live? Biographer Maynard Solomon writes that Mozart's musical forms may be "emblematic, not only of a return to innocence but of the repair of every possible kind of fractured wholeness— a healing of woundedness, a balm to a convalescent soul. . . ."[14] Perhaps this explains why one remarkable pianist and musician, a man who in his youth had championed and performed demanding contemporary works, played only Mozart in his later years. He said it gave him all he needed.

It is poignant to realize that in his last year, when he composed *The Magic Flute*, Mozart's health was poor. He had borrowed money from many of his friends, and his commissions were unworthy of his genius. Was he sustained, as we are, by the music that continued to pour forth? On his deathbed it is said he asked his wife and friends to sing parts of his unfinished *Requiem*, which became his own memorial.

With music like this in our lives, we have a constant friend, whose capacity to give is as near to infinite as anything in this world. One day we may realize that what we were doing all along, as we created a home and family, friendships, and meaningful work, was cultivating an inner garden, a place to commune with what is most loving and eternal in the soul.

MUSIC BREAKS

A Love Letter

Listen to the Brahms Intermezzo, Op. 118, No. 2,* marked *teneramente* (tenderly). Let yourself be rocked by the comforting pulse of this music. Each time the opening theme is repeated it has slightly altered dynamics or harmonies, as if Brahms is trying out different schemes. The reverential organlike passage halfway through the piece may take you into a church for a few moments. If this music arouses longing, explore the nature of your desire. Is it directed toward another, toward work or some desired end, or is it more generalized?

Catching the Joy as It Flies

Listen to the Schumann *Arabesque,* which could have been a wedding present to Clara. It is characteristic of the rondo form to bring back the initial theme after each new section, and with each intervening episode, you can hear the theme gather meaning. Some episodes are passionate and extroverted (in the style of Florestan); others are dreamy and hesitant (in the style of Eusebius). With which personality do you resonate most?

Entering the Garden

Listen to the sublime Adagio from Mozart's Violin Concerto, No. 3, in G major, K. 216,* noticing the simplicity of the repeated pulsing notes in the orchestra that highlight the soaring violin melody. This music is an invitation to enjoy each moment of the journey, an invitation to "Take off your shoes and come into the garden." Notice any imagery the music stimulates. If there are obstacles that make you feel a resistance to the music, try to name or draw them.

Angels' Voices

If you can steal an hour, listen to the entire Fauré *Requiem*. If you have just a few minutes, listen to the conclusion, "In Paradisum,"* a prayer for peace and rest, with no harsh references to a day of judgment. You can always choose to end the day with beauty and harmony.

Sound Journeys:
A Listening Bibliography

RECOMMENDED LISTENING (DISCUSSED IN
TEXT BUT NOT ON CDS)

J. S. Bach: B minor Mass, *St. Matthew Passion,* Unaccompanied Cello Suites (all six, Casals especially recommended),
Goldberg Variations, Italian Concerto, Partitas and Suites
for keyboard, *Brandenburg Concerti,* Christmas Oratorio,
cantatas and passions

Beethoven: Trio in B-flat, Opus 97 (the Archduke); the five
piano concerti; sonatas for cello and piano (try for the
Du Prés and Barenboim recording); piano sonatas, especially *Pathétique, Appassionata,* and Opus 109, 110, and
111; string quartets, especially the late ones, Opus 127 to
Opus 135; Symphonies No. 3, 5, 7, and 9

Brahms: Violin Concerto, intermezzi for piano

Debussy: *Prelude to the Afternoon of a Faun*

Haydn: *Lord Nelson Mass, The Creation*

Mozart: *Requiem,* string quartets and quintets, piano sonatas and concerti, sonatas for violin and piano (Perlman and Barenboim) Clarinet Concerto, K. 633

MUSIC FOR STIMULATING IMAGERY

Canteloube: *Songs of the Auvergne*

Copland: *Appalachian Spring*

Debussy: orchestral works: *Nocturnes, Prelude to the After-noon of a Faun, Dances Sacred and Profane, La Mer,* the string quartet, "The Engulfed Cathedral" for piano

Holst: *The Planets* (many moods and categories, from upbeat Jupiter to mystic Neptune)

Hovhaness: *Mysterious Mountain*

Mussorgski-Ravel: "Great Gate at Kiev" from *Pictures at an Exhibition*

Nakai, Carlos: *Cycles* (Native American flute music)

Narada artists: *A Childhood Remembered*

Rachmaninoff: *Rhapsody on a Theme by Paganini* (piano and orchestra)

Ravel: the string quartet, Piano Concerto for the Left Hand, *Daphnis and Chloé,* Suite 2

Respighi: *Pines of Rome, Fountains of Rome*

Vaughan Williams: *Fantasia on a Theme by Thomas Tallis,* Serenade to Music, first movement of Symphony No. 3 (Pastoral), Symphony No. 5

Vivaldi: *The Four Seasons*
Wagner: Siegfried Idyll

MUSIC FOR MEDITATION AND REFLECTION

Bach: Arioso from Cantata 156, *St. Matthew Passion*, B minor Mass, Adagio from Concerto No. 2 in E minor for Violin and Strings

Beethoven: second movement of Piano Concerto No. 5 (the *Emperor*), Andante and Adagio movements of sonatas

Brahms: second movement of Piano Concerto No. 1; Intermezzo, Opus 118, No. 2; *A German Requiem*

Bruckner: third movement of Symphony No. 8

Chopin: slow movement of Piano Concerto No. 1

Cornysh, William: *Stabat Mater* (Tallis Scholars)

Couperin, François: *Les Leçons des Ténèbres* (for women's voices)

Fauré: sections of the *Requiem*

Gounod: Sanctus from *St. Cecilia's Mass*

Gregorian Chant and early music by Hildegard of Bingen, Josquin des Pres, Palestrina and others

Händel: Largo movements from the operas

Paul Horn: *Inside the Taj Mahal*

Lauridsen: *Lux Aeterna* (Calm, luminous, music as prayer)

Les Voix Humaines, selected works for viola da gamba, played by Jordi Savall

Mahler: Adagietto from Symphony No. 5

Monteverdi: *Vespers of the Blessed Virgin, Laudate Dominum*

Mozart: *Ave Verum Corpus,* the *Requiem,* Andante and Adagio movements from symphonies and concerti

Pachelbel: Canon in D

Schubert: slower movements from symphonies or string quartets, songs (especially "Ave Maria")

Thomas Tallis: *Spem in alium* and other sacred pieces

Vaughan Williams: *Fantasia on a Theme of Thomas Tallis, The Lark Ascending, Serenade to Music*

Wagner: Prelude to Act I of *Lohengrin;* Prelude, Good Friday, and descent of the Grail from *Parsifal*

OTHER COLLECTIONS:

Deuter: with Annette Cantor, *Garden of the Gods* (numinous vocal serenades)

Peter Kater: *Compassion,* with David Darling and others (beautiful and heart-opening)

Kamal: *Into Silence*

Lauren Pomerantz: *Tree of Life* (original songs based on the Kabbalah)

Nóirín Ní Riain and the monks of Glenstal Abbey: *Vox de Nube*

Steve Roach: *Quiet Music*

David Sun: *The Secret Garden*

Master Charles: *The Sounds of Source*, from Synchronicity Foundation, Inc.

MUSIC TO QUICKEN ENERGY (ALSO, SEE
LISTINGS UNDER FIRE)

Bach: *Brandenburg Concerti, Leipzig Sonatas,* and faster
dances from the suites and partitas for keyboard and for
unaccompanied violin and cello, violin concerti

Beethoven: *Egmont Overture, Lenore Overture,* outer movements of piano trios and Piano Concerti No. 4 and No. 5,
final movement of Symphonies No. 7 and (especially)
No. 9; final movement of the Archduke Trio, Opus 97;
first movement of the Violin Concerto; Scherzo of Symphony No. 3 (the *Eroica)*

Brahms: Violin Concerto (first and last movements), piano
concerti, and Hungarian dances and rhapsodies

Chopin: Polonaise in A-flat, Opus 53

Clementi: sonatas for piano (played by Horowitz or Maria
Tipo)

Mahler: first and second movements of First Symphony,
first movement of Eighth Symphony, and final movement of Third Symphony

Marcello: recorder concerti

Mozart: allegro and presto movements of symphonies and
trios, especially No. 41 (the Jupiter), overtures to *The
Marriage of Figaro* and *The Magic Flute,* horn concerti

Mendelssohn: *Italian* Symphony, Violin Concerto

Purcell: "Sound the Trumpet" and other secular songs

Rachmaninoff: final movement of Piano Concerto No. 2, the Sonata for Piano and Cello

Schumann: Fantasy for Piano, Opus 17; Symphony No. 3 (the Rhenish)

Tchaikovsky: Violin Concerto, faster movements from symphonies

OTHER COLLECTIONS:

O'Connor, Ma, and Myers: *Appalachian Waltz* (a collaboration between a virtuoso fiddler, cellist, and bassist)

Martin Hayes and Dennis Cahill: *The Lonesome Touch* (a superb Irish fiddler and guitarist playing Irish reels and laments)

Paco Peña: Playing flamenco guitar music of Montoya and Ricardo

MUSIC OF PARADISE, MYSTERY, AND TRANSCENDENCE

Bach: Arioso (heartbreaking beauty, transpersonal)

Bartók: Adagio religioso from the No. 3 Piano Concerto

Beethoven: Cavatina from String Quartet in B-flat, Opus 130; Lento movement of String Quartet, Opus 135; Andante cantabile of the Archduke Trio, Opus 97; Adagio of Symphony No. 9; first movement of Symphony No. 6 (Pastorale)

Bernstein, Leonard: "Adonai" from *Chichester Psalms*

Brahms: Violin Concerto (second movement), Four Songs for Voices, Horn and Harp, Opus 17

Debussy: *Prelude to the Afternoon of a Faun*, "Sirens" from *Nocturnes*

Dvořák: Largo from *New World Symphony*

Elgar, Edward: Nimrod variation (9th) from *Enigma Variations*

Fauré: "In Paradisum" from the *Requiem*

Gorecki: Third Symphony, *Miserere*

Gounod: Sanctus from *St. Cecilia's Mass*

Händel: *Water Music* and *Royal Fireworks*

Lauridsen: *Lux Aeterna*

Mahler: *Rückert Lieder*

Mendelssohn: Andante from the String Symphony No. 4, Incidental music from *A Midsummer Night's Dream*

Messaien: *Visions of Amen, Quartet for the End of Time*

Mozart: Andante and Adagio movements, especially from the Clarinet Concerto, K. 622, and Piano Concerto No. 21; Concerto for Flute and Harp; *Vesperae Solemnes de Confessore; Laudate Dominum*

Part, Arvo: *Te Deum, Tabula Rasa, Cantus for Benjamin Britten*

Raatavara: *Angel of Light*

Rachmaninoff: *Vespers,* Cello Sonata

Schubert: songs, including "An die Musik" (To Music), "Nacht und Träume" (Night and Dreams), and "Du bist

die Ruhe"; G-flat major Impromptu, Opus 90; slow
movements from piano sonatas and string quartets
Strauss, Richard: Transfiguration from *Death and Transfig-
uration* and *Late Songs* (if possible, sung by Schwarzkopf)
Tavener, John: *The Protecting Veil* and *Eternity's Sunrise*
Tchaikovsky: *Serenade in C*
Vaughan Williams: *Serenade to Music* and *The Lark Ascending*

OTHER COLLECTIONS:

Deuter: *Garden of the Gods*
Hillyard Ensemble: *Officium* (early music for chorus, with
soulful improvisations by saxophonist Jan Garbarek)
Sacred Treasures: Choral Masterworks from Russia

SENSUAL MUSIC

The Astrud Gilberto Album (Verve label)
Andrea Bocelli: *Romanza,* especially "Per Amore"
Getz/Gilberto: *The Girl from Ipanema*
Keith Jarrett: *The Köln Concert*
Modern Jazz Quartet: *No Sun in Venice*
Pat Metheny and Charlie Haden: *Beyond the Missouri Sky*
and *Jim Hall and Pat Metheny*
Piazzola: *Hommage to Piazzola* (tangos)
Rachmaninoff: Adagio from Piano Concerto No. 2, Adagio
from Symphony No. 2, the song "Vocalise."

Tchaikovsky: Canzonetta from *Violin Concerto*

Tuck and Patty: *Tears of Joy*

Villa-Lobos: *Bachianas Brasileiras*, No. 5

Denny Zeitlin: jazz piano with David Friesen, bass, on the Concord label

MUSIC FOR STUDYING AND WORKING

Bach: Orchestral Suites and *Brandenburg Concerti*

Baroque music: slow movements of Bach, Telemann, Vivaldi, Corelli, and other Italian masters

Celtic harp: Alan Stivell, Patrick Ball, and others

Classical guitar collections: by Julian Bream, Christopher Parkening, Andrés Segovia, and John Williams

Enya: quiet vocals

Gregorian chants: the Choir of St. Peter's Abbey, Solesmes; and early music collections by groups such as the Anonymous Four, Hesperian XX (Jordi Savall), Hilliard Ensemble, Sequentia, and Tallis Scholars

Händel: *Water Music*

Haydn: string quartets

MUSIC OF THE ELEMENTS

EARTH. TO SUPPORT A FULL RANGE OF EMOTIONS, LOVE, LONGING, JOY, AND PAIN. FOR GROUNDING AFTER MUSIC OF AIR, WATER, OR FIRE.

Bach: selected movements from Unaccompanied Cello Suites

Beethoven: Largo from Piano Sonata, Opus 10, No. 3; Symphony No. 6 (Pastorale); selected movements (especially second and third movements of No. 3, No. 6, and No. 7); piano sonatas

Brahms: first movement of Horn Trio, Opus 40; *A German Requiem* (sacred earth music); Symphony No. 1; Two Songs, Opus 91, for Viola and Soprano; Intermezzi for piano; cello sonatas; piano concerti; Andante from Concerto for Violin, Cello and Orchestra in A minor; third movement of Symphony No. 4

Dvořák: Symphony No. 7, Piano Quartet, Op. 87

Granados: *Spanish Dances* (folk dances for piano)

Holst: Saturn, from *The Planets*

Orff: *Carmina Burana* (cathartic, dramatic, and strongly rhythmic)

Rachmaninoff: "Vocalise" and other songs; Piano Concerto No. 2; Prelude, Opus 32, in B minor

Russian songs: the CD, *My Restless Soul,* sung by Dmitri Hvorostovsky

Savall, Jordi: *Les Voix Humaines,* early music selections for viola da gamba (heart-opening)

Schumann: selections from *Kreisleriana, Carnival, Davids-bündlertänze,* and other piano collections

Sibelius: Symphony No. 4 (especially first movement)

Tchaikovsky: Serenade for Orchestra in C major, Opus 48; String Sextet, Opus 70 *(Souvenir de Florence)*

OTHER COLLECTIONS:

BeauSoleil: *L'Echo* (Cajun)

Dave Brubeck: *Time Out* and *Time Further Out*

Drumming collections by Mickey Hart, Olatunji, and others

Eugene Friesen: *New Friend* (cello)

Keith Jarrett: the *Köln Concert* (a jazz piano classic)

Brad Mehldau: *Elegiac Cycle* (piano, classically inspired)

WATER. TO ENCOURAGE ASSOCIATIVE, DREAMY, SENSUAL REVERIE AND UNCONSCIOUS EMOTIONS. REFRESHING AND COOLING AFTER EARTH OR FIRE.

Bach: works for the lute

Beethoven: Andante molto moto movement (the scene by the brook) from Symphony No. 6 (Pastorale)

Britten: Four Sea Interludes from *Peter Grimes*

Chopin: Nocturne Opus 49, No. 1, *Barcarolle*

Debussy: "La Mer," string quartet, keyboard works such as "Reflections on the Water," "Ondine, The Engulfed Cathedral," "Gardens in the Rain," "Fish of Gold"

Fauré: Nocturnes and Barcarolles for piano (Sensuous and evocative)

Liszt: *Les Jeux d'eau à la Villa d'Este*

Picker, Tobias: *Old and Lost Rivers*

Ravel: *Ondine, Jeux d'eau,* "Pavane for a Dead Princess"

Respighi: Appian Way from *Pines of Rome*

Saint-Saëns: *The Swan*

Smetana: *The Moldau*

Schubert: G-flat and A-flat Impromptus, Opus 90, for piano; string quintet (the Trout)

Strauss, Johann: *The Beautiful Blue Danube*

Thomson, Virgil: *The River*

Tarrega: *Recuerdos de la Alhambra* (evocative memories of water in the gardens of Granada, Spain)

Vivaldi: suites for mandolin and guitar

FIRE. TO INCREASE THE TEMPERATURE OF PASSION AND CREATIVITY. ENERGIZING AT ANY TIME.

J. S. Bach: Gloria from B minor Mass, *Brandenburg Concerti,* toccatas for keyboard (especially the D minor)

Bartók: *Music for Strings, Percussion and Celesta,* Piano Concerto No. 2, String Quartet No. 3

Beethoven: Scherzo movements in the Symphony No. 3 (the *Eroica),* first movement of Symphony No. 5, first movement of Piano Sonata No. 32, Opus 111, faster movements of quartets and sonatas

Brahms: Gypsy music, as in the final movement of the Violin Concerto, *Hungarian Dances,* rhapsodies, and *Rondo alla Zingarese* of Piano Quartet in G minor, Opus 25

de Falla: *Ritual Fire Dance, El Amor Brujo*

Dvořák: Piano Trio in E minor (the Dumky) and B-flat Piano Concerto, No. 1

Philip Glass: The Grid from *Koyaanisqatsi*

Granados: selected *Spanish Dances* (piano)

Liszt: Etude transcendante in F minor

Mozart: overture to *The Marriage of Figaro*, first movement of Symphony No. 41 (the Jupiter)

Rachmaninoff: third movement of Piano Concerto No. 2

Shostakovich: Scherzo from the Piano Quintet in G minor, Opus 57

Sibelius: Violin Concerto

Stravinsky: *Firebird* and *Rite of Spring*

Tchaikovsky: Violin Concerto

Verdi: "Sempre libera" from *La Traviata* and other selected arias; the *Requiem*

Wagner: Magic Fire music from *Die Walküre*

OTHER COLLECTIONS

Flamenco guitar music of Ramón Montoya, Nino Ricardo, Paco Peña, Bob Weisenberg (the CD *American Gypsy*).

AIR. TO ENCOURAGE SPIRIT, IMAGINATION, AND INTUITION. UPLIFTING.

Bach: B minor Sonata (for flute and keyboard)

Debussy: *Prelude to the Afternoon of a Faun;* Nuages (Clouds) from *Nocturnes;* Sonata for Flute, Viola and Harp; Rhapsody No. 1 for Clarinet and Piano

Fauré: In Paradisum from the *Requiem*

Gluck: *Dance of the Blessed Spirits*

Harrison, Lou: selections from *La Koro Sutro* (musical settings of Buddhist sutras)

Holst: Uranus, from *The Planets*

Lauridsen: *Lux Aeterna*

Ligeti: *Requiem* and *Lux Aeterna* (on *2001: A Space Odyssey* soundtrack)

Mendelssohn: *A Midsummer Night's Dream*

Mozart: Clarinet Concerto, K. 622 (especially the second movement), chamber music for winds

Ravel: "Pavane for a Dead Princess"

Vaughan Williams: *The Lark Ascending*

Wagner: Prelude to Acts I and III of *Lohengrin,* Prelude to Act I of *Parsifal*

OTHER COLLECTIONS:

Don Campbell: *Angels and Essence* (original compositions)

Kelly-Halpern: *Ancient Echoes*

Paul Horn: *Inside the Taj Mahal*

Michael Hoppé and Tim Wheater: *The Yearning* (romances for alto flute)

Lauren Pomerantz: *Tree of Life*

Raphael: *Music to Disappear In*

Richard Stoltzman: *Spirit* (virtuoso clarinet)

Vangelis: *Icarus*

MY DESERT ISLAND CHOICES

Bach: B minor Mass, *Magnificat, Goldberg Variations,* Arioso from Cantata 156, Air on a G String from the Third Suite, the B-flat Partita for (keyboard), Unaccompanied Cello Suites

Beethoven: Archduke Trio, Opus 97; the late string quartets and late piano sonatas; Symphonies No. 7 and No 9

Brahms: B major Piano Trio, Opus 8; Intermezzi for piano

Mozart: *Don Giovanni;* the string quintets; sonatas for piano and violin; Trio for Piano, Clarinet, and Viola, K. 498; Clarinet Concerto, K. 622; the A minor Piano Sonata, K. 310; Fantasy and Sonata in C minor, K. 475 and 457; Piano Concerti: D minor, K. 466, B-flat, K. 595; and C major, K. 503; Symphonies 39, 40, and 41

Rachmaninoff: Sonata for Piano and Cello

Schubert: String Quintet in C, D. 56; Sonata in B-flat, D. 960; songs, "Nacht und Träume" and "Du Bist die Ruhe"

Schumann: Fantasy in C, Opus 17

A Musical Toolkit

Choose your six favorite tapes or CDs and list them below. Across from each one put down one or two words about how this music makes you feel. Keep these selections close by, for special times.

Musical Terms

arpeggio: a chord with the notes played one after the other in rapid succession rather than simultaneously.

aria: a composition for solo singer or instrumentalist and accompaniment.

atonal: the absence of a tonal center.

cadence: a pause or stopping point.

chord: a vertical combination of tones heard or played simultaneously.

coda: the concluding section of a piece.

consonance: intervals or chords that sound relatively stable.

counterpoint: the playing of simultaneous, distinctive musical lines.

crescendo: to gradually get louder.

decrescendo: to gradually get softer.

development: the process of expanding themes and motives into larger sections of music.

diminution: presenting a subject in shorter note values.

dissonance: intervals or chords that sound relatively unstable.

dynamics: the loudness or softness of pitch.

entrainment: the tendency of a stronger rhythm to draw a weaker one into resonance with it.

exposition: the first section of a sonata form movement.

fugue: a composition written in imitative counterpoint, based on a theme (subject) which is stated at the beginning in one voice and then taken up (imitated) by other voices. Each fugue also contains episodes in which the subject is not being stated.

galant style: the light, popular, elegant musical style of the later eighteenth century.

gavotte: a French dance in quick duple time.

harmonics: the secondary pitches that sound above the fundamental note being struck or sounded.

harmony: the relationships tones form with one another. Also refers to the vertical aspects or chords of a musical texture.

interval: the distance between two tones, measured by the number of scale notes between them.

learned style: composition using counterpoint.

major mode: a scale of whole tones, except for half steps between the third and fourth and the seventh and eighth tones.

measure: a group of beats marked off on the score by a vertical line.

melismas: segments of melody that are sung on a single note.

melody: a succession of pitches with a meaningful musical shape.

meter: a grouping of beats into stressed and unstressed units, in a regular, repeating pattern.

minimalism: a late twentieth-century style that involves many repetitions of musical fragments.

minor mode: a scale characterized by the interval between the first and third notes in which there are three half-steps rather than four, as in the major mode.

minuet: a popular dance in triple meter of the seventeenth and eighteenth centuries.

octave: duplicate notes, eight notes apart.

overtone: the secondary vibrations which contribute to the tone color.

pentatonic scale: the five black notes beginning with F-sharp on the piano. Widely used in folk music.

pitch: the number of vibrations that determine the highness or lowness of a sound.

pizzicato: plucking the strings with the fingers.

polyphony: music in which two or more lines are played simultaneously.

recapitulation: the third section of a sonata-form movement, in which the material of the exposition is presented in the home key.

rhythm: the aspect of music that generates, measures, organizes, and controls time.

ritardando: slowing down the tempo.

rondo: a piece consisting of one main theme that alternates with other themes or sections.

scherzo: a quick, dancelike movement that Beethoven developed to replace the minuet. Also used alone by Chopin.

sonata: a work of three or more movements in alternating tempos.

sonata form: the most important form of the Classic era, involving a long-range harmonic plan in which each key area has distinctive themes.

tempo: the pace or speed of music.

timbre: the tone color of a voice or instrument, which affects its sonorous quality.

tonality: the organization of music around the centrality of one note.

trill: an ornamental figure consisting of two adjacent notes played rapidly in alternation.

Endnotes

INTRODUCTION

1. From "Mythological Themes in Creative Literature and Art," in *Myths, Dreams, and Religion*, edited by Joseph Campbell (New York: Dutton & Co., Inc., 1970), 148.
2. Saint Augustine, *The Confessions* (New York: Penguin Books, 1961), 231–32.

CHAPTER I: THE HEART OF LISTENING

1. *Sonnets to Orpheus, Duino Elegies*, translated by Ted Andersson and Kenneth Fields.

CHAPTER II: HEARING THE DESIGN

1. As in the "Arioso" in the Piano Sonata No. 32 (Opus 110), in the Hammerklavier sonata (Opus 106), in the Diabelli Variations, in the *Grosse Fugue*, and in the last movements of the Third and Ninth Symphonies.
2. Sogyal Rinpoche, *The Tibetan Book of Living and Dying* (San Francisco: HarperSan Francisco, 1992), 143.

CHAPTER III: THE EDUCATION OF FEELING

1. George Bernard Shaw, "The Religion of the Pianoforte," *Fortnightly Review*, reprinted in the anthology *Words on Music*, edited by Jack Sullivan (Athens, Ohio: Ohio University Press, 1990).

CHAPTER IV: WHEN YOU ARE THE MUSIC

1. Marcel Proust, *Swann's Way*, trans. C. K. Scott Moncrieff (New York: Heritage Press, 1954), 362*ff.*

2. R. H. Blyth, *Zen and Zen Classics*, vol. 5 (Tokyo: Hokuseido Press, 1962), 112. A poet and writer, Blyth was the English tutor of the Japanese Crown Prince.

3. Howard Nemerov, "Lines & Circularities," in *Gnomes & Occasions* (Chicago: University of Chicago Press, 1973).

4. Alla Renée Bozarth, excerpt from "What Is Prayer?" in *Moving to the Edge of the World*, iuniverse.com, 2000.

CHAPTER V: SINGING YOUR OWN SONG

1. John Moyne and Coleman Barks, *Open Secret* (Putney, Vermont: Threshold Books, 1984).

2. Wallace Stevens, "The Idea of Order at Key West," *The Palm at the End of the Mind* (New York: Vintage Books, 1972).

3. Maria Leach, *The Beginning: Creation Myths Around the World* (New York: Funk and Wagnall, 1956).

4. Joscelyn Godwin, *Harmonies of Heaven and Earth* (Rochester, Vermont: Inner Traditions International, Ltd., 1987), 60.

5. In his preface to Wilson's *The Miraculous Birth of Language*.

6. Diane M. Clark, "Professor Turned Healer," in *Open Ear*, vol. 3, 1997, a publication directed by Pat Moffitt Cook, dedicated to sound and music in health and education. Box 10276, Bainbridge Island, WA 98110.

7. Angel's CD *Chant*, sung by the Benedictine monks of Santo Domingo de Silos in Spain, has sold over two million copies since the spring of 1994.

CHAPTER VI: THE ALCHEMY OF MUSIC

1. Reported in the journal for the Center for Frontier Studies at Temple University, v. 8, No. 1, Spring, 1999.

2. See Melinda Maxfield's "The Journey of the Drum," in *Music and Miracles*, compiled by Don G. Campbell (Wheaton, Ill.: Quest Books, Theosophical Publishing House, 1992).

3. Thomas Moore, *The Planets Within* (Hudson, N.Y.: Lindisfarne Press, 1990).

4. Henry Dreher, *The Immune Power Personality* (New York: Penguin Plume, 1996), 34.

5. See Sheila Ostrander and Lynn Schroeder, *Superlearning* and the work of Lozanov about using music to improve and speed up learning.

CHAPTER VII: THE HEALING POWER OF MUSIC

1. Mary Oliver, *Winter Hours* (Boston and New York: Houghton Mifflin, 1999), 106.

2. It may be ordered from Songbird Music, 2977 Ygnacio Valley Rd., #144, Walnut Creek, Calif. 94598, or e-mail: Laurenpom@aol.com

3. His Holiness the Dalai Lama and Howard C. Cutler, *The Art of Happiness* (New York: Riverhead, 1998), p. 254.

4. Alfred Einstein, *Mozart* (New York: Oxford University Press, 1945), 192.

5. Rainer Maria Rilke, *Letters to a Young Poet* (New York: Norton, 1934), 64.

6. Ibid., 7.

7. Oliver Sacks, *A Leg to Stand On* (New York: Summit Books, 1984), 148–49.

8. "The Healing Power of Music," in the *BBC Music Magazine*, April 1996.

9. You may read more about Therese Schroeder-Sheker's mission and practice in her article in *Sonic Alchemy* by Joshua Leeds (Sausalito, Calif: InnerSong Press, 1997).

CHAPTER VIII: DREAMING AND DANCING

1. Michael Tippett, *Moving into Aquarius* (London: Paladin Books, 1984), 156.

2. "The Uses of Poetry and the Uses of Criticism," *Selected Prose of T. S. Eliot*, edited by Frank Kermode (New York: Harcourt Brace Jovanovich, 1975).

3. *Memories, Dreams, and Reflections* (New York: Vintage Books, 1965), 177.

4. Leonard Bernstein, *The Infinite Variety of Music* (New York: Simon and Schuster, 1966).

5. From "Music" in *Fourteen Sonnets by Baudelaire,* tr. Walter Martin, (El Cerrito, Calif: Jacaranda Press, 1991).

6. Rumi, 281.

CHAPTER IX: THE INNER GARDEN

1. In German the motto reads in full: *Durch alle Tone tonet / Im bunten Erdentraum / Ein leiser Ton gezogen / Für den, der heimlich lauschet.*

2. George Herbert, "The Temper," in *Seventeenth-Century Prose and Poetry,* ed. by Robert Tristram Coffin and Alexander Witherspoon (New York: Harcourt, Brace and Company, 1946).

3. C. G. Jung, in *The Spirit in Man, Art, and Literature. Collected Works,* vol. 15, pars. 97–132.

4. Styra Avins, *Johannes Brahms, Life and Letters* (Oxford and New York: Oxford University Press, 1997), 72.

5. Roland Barthes, "Loving Schumann" and "Rasch," in *The Responsibility of Forms,* trans. by Richard Howard (Berkeley and Los Angeles: University of California Press, 1991).

6. C. A. Meier, *Soul and Body* (San Francisco: Lapis Press, 1986), 204*ff.*

7. Gemisthus Pletho, in Germain Bazin, *Paradeisos: The Art of the Garden* (Toronto: Bullfinch Press, Little, Brown & Company, 1990), 63.

8. Celia Thaxter, *An Island Garden* (Boston: Houghton Mifflin, 1894), and the beautiful edition of 1988, with pictures and illuminations by Childe Hassam.

9. Lawrence Weschler, "Inventing Peace," *The New Yorker,* November 20, 1995.

10. *The Kabir Book,* versions by Robert Bly (Boston: Seventies Press Book, Beacon Press, 1971).

11. In David Blum, *Casals and the Art of Interpretation* (Berkeley and Los Angeles: University of California Press, 1977), 7.

12. Don Campbell, *The Mozart Effect* (New York: Avon Books, 1997).

13. Antony Hopkins, *Understanding Music* (New York: Oxford University Press, 1993), 178.

14. Maynard Solomon, *Mozart* (New York: HarperCollins, 1995), 197.

Bibliography

Saint Augustine. *Confessions*. New York: Penguin, 1961.

Avins, Styra. *Johannes Brahms, Life and Letters*. New York: Oxford University Press, 1997.

Bachelard, Gaston. *The Poetics of Reverie*. Boston: Beacon Press, 1960.

Barthes, Roland. "Loving Schumann" and "Rasch," in *The Responsibility of Forms*. Trans. Richard Howard. Berkeley: University of California Press, 1991.

Baudelaire, Charles. *Fourteen Sonnets*. Trans. Walter Martin. El Cerrito, Calif.: Jacaranda Press, 1991.

Bazin, Germain. *Paradeisos: The Art of the Garden*. Toronto: Bullfinch Press, Little, Brown & Company, 1990.

Bernstein, Leonard. *The Joy of Music*. New York: Simon and Schuster, 1959.

———. *The Infinite Variety of Music*. New York: Simon and Schuster, 1962.

———. *Findings*. New York: Simon and Schuster, reprinted by Anchor Books, 1982.

Blum, David. *Casals and the Art of Interpretation*. Berkeley: University of California, 1977.

Bly, Robert, editor. *Selected Poems of Rainer Maria Rilke*. New York: Harper and Row, 1981.

Blyth, R. H. *Zen and Zen Classics*. Tokyo: Hokuseido Press, 1962.

———. *Haiku: Eastern Culture*. Vol. I. Tokyo: Hokuseido Press, 1949.

Bonny, Helen L., and Louis M. Savary. *Music and Your Mind*. New York: Station Hill Press, 1973.

Bozarth, Alla Renée. In *Life Prayers*. Ed. Elizabeth Roberts and Elias Amidon. San Francisco: HarperSan Francisco, 1996.

Brown, Maurice. *Schubert: A Critical Biography*. New York: Da Capo Press, 1977.

Brown, Norman O. *Life Against Death*. New York: Vintage Books, 1959.

———. *Love's Body*. Vintage Books, 1966.

Campbell, Don. *Music Physician for Times to Come*. Wheaton, Ill.: Quest Books, 1991.

———. *Music and Miracles*. Wheaton, Ill.: Quest Books, 1992.

————. *The Mozart Effect*. New York: Avon Books, 1997.

Campbell, Joseph, ed. *Myths, Dreams, and Religion*. New York: Dutton & Co., Inc., 1970.

Clynes, Manfred. *Sentics: The Touch of the Emotions*. New York: Avery Publishing, 1989. Revised edition by Prism Press, Dorset, England.

Copland, Aaron. *Music and Imagination*. Cambridge, Mass.: Harvard University Press, 1952.

————. *What to Listen for in Music*. New York: Mentor Books, 1952.

Corbin, Henry. *Alone with the Alone*. Princeton, N.J.: Bollingen Series, Princeton University Press, 1969.

Dalai Lama and Howard Cutler. *The Art of Happiness*. New York: Riverhead Books, 1998.

Dewey, John. *Art as Experience*. New York: Perigee Books, Berkeley Publishing Group, 1934.

Dickinson, Emily. *The Complete Poems*. Ed. Thomas H. Johnson. Boston: Little Brown and Company, 1976.

Dreher, Henry. *The Immune Power Personality: Seven Traits You Can Develop to Stay Healthy*. New York: Penguin Books, 1995.

Edinger, Edward F. *Anatomy of the Psyche*. La Salle, Ill.: Open Court Publishing, 1985.

Einstein, Albert. *Mozart*. New York: Oxford University Press, 1945.

Eliot, T. S., "The Uses of Poetry and the Uses of Criticism." In *Selected Prose of T. S. Eliot*. Ed. Frank Kermode. New York: Harcourt Brace Jovanovich, 1975.

————. *Four Quartets*. New York: Harcourt, Brace & World, Inc., 1942.

Farrell, Kate. *Art and Wonder*. New York: Metropolitan Museum of Art, 1996.

Gaynor, Mitchell L. *Sounds of Healing*. New York: Broadway Books, Random House, 1999.

Godwin, Joscelyn, ed. *Cosmic Music*. Rochester, Vt.: Inner Traditions, 1989.

————. *Harmonies of Heaven and Earth*. Rochester, Vt.: Inner Traditions, 1987.

————. *The Mystery of the Seven Vowels*. Grand Rapids, Mich.: Phanes Press, 1991.

Goleman, Daniel, ed. *Healing Emotions*. Boston: Shambhala Publications, Inc., 1997.

Hamel, Peter Michael. *Through Music to the Self*. Dorset, England: Element Books, Ltd., 1978.

Herbert, George. "The Temper." *Seventeenth-Century Prose and Poetry*. Ed. Robert Tristram Coffin and Alexander Witherspoon. New York: Harcourt, Brace and Company, 1946.

Heschel, Abraham. *I Asked for Wonder*. Ed. Samuel H. Dresner. New York: Crossroad, 1985.

Hindemith, Paul. *Johann Sebastian Bach*. New Haven: Yale University Press, 1952.

Hopkins, Antony. *Understanding Music*. New York: Oxford University Press, 1993.

Johnson, Robert A. *Inner Work: Using Dreams and Active Imagination for Personal Growth*. San Francisco: Harper & Row, 1986.

Jourdain, Robert. *Music, the Brain, and Ecstasy*. New York: William Morrow and Co, Inc., 1997.

Jung, C. G. "The Transcendent Function." In *The Portable Jung*. New York: Viking Press, 1971.

———. *Memories, Dreams, Reflections*. New York: Vintage Books, Random House, 1965.

Kabir. *The Kabir Book*. Versions by Robert Bly. Boston: Seventies Press Book, Beacon Press, 1971.

Kittelson, Mary Lynn. *Sounding the Soul: The Art of Listening*. Einsiedeln, Switzerland: Daimon, 1996.

Khan, Hazrat Inayat. *The Mysticism of Sound and Music*. Boston and London: Shambhala Dragon Editions, 1996.

Leach, Maria. *The Beginning: Creation Myths Around the World*. New York: Funk and Wagnall, 1956.

Leeds, Joshua. *Sonic Alchemy*. Sausalito, Calif.: Innersong Press, 1997.

Le Mée, Katharine, *Chant: The Origins, Form, Practice, and Healing Power of Gregorian Chant*. New York: Bell Tower, 1994.

Margolis, Victor. *The Plate Spinner*. Cupertino, Calif.: Marik Publishing, 1995.

Mathieu, W. A. *The Listening Book: Discovering Your Own Music*. Boston and London: Shambhala, 1991.

———. *The Musical Life*. Boston and London: Shambhala, 1994.

Meier, C. A. *Soul and Body*. San Francisco: Lapis Press, 1986.

Mellick, Jill. *The Natural Artistry of Dreams*. Berkeley, Calif.: Conari Press, 1996.

Merritt, Stephanie. *Mind, Music and Imagery*. New York: Plume, Penguin, 1991.

Meyer, Leonard B. *Emotion and Meaning in Music*. Chicago: University of Chicago, 1956.

Miles, Russell H. *Johann Sebastian Bach*. Englewood Cliffs, N.J.: Prentice-Hall, Inc., 1962.

Moore, Thomas. *The Care of the Soul*. New York: HarperPerennial, a division of HarperCollins, 1992.

———. *The Re-Enchantment of Everyday Life*. New York: HarperCollins, 1996.

———. *The Planets Within*. Hudson, N.Y.: Lindisfarne Press, 1990.

Mozart, W. A. *Letters of Wolfgang Amadeus Mozart*. Ed. Hans Mersmann, New York: Dover, 1972.

Nemerov, Howard. "Lines & Circularities." In *Gnomes & Occasions*. Chicago: University of Chicago Press, 1973.

Oliver, Mary. *Winter Hours*. Boston and New York: Houghton Mifflin Company, 1999.

Ostrander, Sheila, and Lynn Schroeder. *Superlearning*. New York: Dell, 1979.

Ostwald, Peter. *Schumann: the Inner Voices of a Musical Genius*. Boston: Northeastern University Press, 1985.

Proust, Marcel. *Swann's Way*. Trans. C. K. Scott Moncrieff. New York: Heritage Press, 1954.

Rider, Mark. *The Rhythmic Language of Health and Disease*. MMB Music, 1997.

Rilke, Rainer Maria. *Letters to a Young Poet*. New York: W. W. Norton & Company, 1934.

————. *Rilke and Benvenuta: An Intimate Correspondence*. Trans. by Joel Agee. New York: Fromm International Publishing Corp., 1987.

————. *The Selected Poetry of Rainer Maria Rilke*. Trans. Stephen Mitchell, New York: Vintage Books, 1984.

Rinpoche, Sogyal. *The Tibetan Book of Living and Dying*. San Francisco: HarperSan Francisco, 1992.

Roberts, Gareth. *The Mirror of Alchemy*. Toronto: University of Toronto Press, 1994.

Roberts, Paul. *Images: the Piano Music of Claude Debussy*, Portland, Ore.: Amadeus Press, 1996.

Rosen, Charles. *The Classical Style: Haydn, Mozart, Beethoven*. New York: W. W. Norton and Co., 1972.

————. *The Romantic Generation*. Cambridge, Mass.: Harvard University Press, 1995.

Rumi. *The Essential Rumi*. Trans. Coleman Barks and John Moyne. San Francisco: HarperSanFrancisco, Calif., 1995.

Sacks, Oliver. *A Leg to Stand On*. New York: HarperCollins, 1984.

Scott-Maxwell, Florida. *The Measure of My Days*. Middlesex, England, and New York: Penguin Books, 1979.

Sessions, Roger. *The Musical Experience of Composer, Performer, Listener*. Princeton, N.J.: Princeton University Press, 1950.

Shaw, George Bernard. "The Religion of the Pianoforte." *Fortnightly Review*. Reprinted in *Words on Music*. Ed. Jack Sullivan. Athens, Ohio: Ohio University Press, 1990.

Slonimsky, Nicolas. *Lexicon of Musical Invective*. Seattle and London: University of Washington Press, 1953.

————. *The Road to Music*. New York: Dodd, Mead and Company, 1966.

Smith, Huston. *The Religions of Man*. New York: Perennial Library, Harper and Row, 1965.

Solomon, Maynard. *Beethoven*. New York: Schirmer, 1977.

————. *Beethoven Essays*. Cambridge, Mass.: Harvard University Press, 1988.

————. *Mozart*. New York: HarperCollins, 1997.

Staudacher, Carol. *A Time to Grieve*. San Francisco: HarperSan Francisco, 1994.

Stevens, Wallace. *The Palm at the End of the Mind*. New York: Vintage Books, 1972.

Storr, Anthony. *Music and the Mind*. New York: Free Press, Macmillan, Inc., 1992.

Sullivan, J.W.N. *Beethoven, His Spiritual Development*. New York: Vintage Books, 1927.

Thaxter, Celia. *An Island Garden*. Boston: Houghton Mifflin, 1894 and 1988.

Thayer, Alexander Wheelock. *Life of Beethoven*. Ed. Elliot Forbes. Revised ed. Princeton, N.J.: Princeton University Press, 1967.

Three Classics in the Aesthetic of Music, Debussy, Ives, and Busoni. New York: Dover, 1962.

Thurman, Robert A. F. *The Essential Tibetan Buddhism*. San Francisco: Harper-San Francisco, 1995.

Tippett, Michael. *Moving into Aquarius*. London: Paladin Books, 1984.

Tomatis, Alfred A. *The Conscious Ear*. Barrytown, New York: Station Hill Press, 1991.

Wilson, Frank R. *Tone Deaf and All Thumbs? An Invitation to Music Making*. Vintage Books, 1986.

Yeats, W. B. *Collected Poems*. New York: Macmillan, 1933.

Zuckerkandl, Victor. *Man the Musician*. Princeton, N.J.: Bollingen Series, Princeton University Press, 1973.

————. *Sound and Symbol*. Princeton, N.J.: Bollingen Series, Princeton University Press, 1956.

————. *The Sense of Music*. Princeton, N.J.: Princeton University Press, 1959.

Credits / Permissions

Wallace Stevens: "The Idea of Order at Key West," from *Collected Poems,* Copyright © 1954 by Wallace Steves. Reprinted by permission of Alfred A. Knopf, a Division of Random House Inc.

Rumi: "Dance, when you're broken open . . ." and "Today, like every other day . . .", *The Essential Rumi,* translated by Coleman Barks, HarperSan Francisco, 1995. Originally published by Threshold Books and reprinted with the permission of Threshold Productions.

Kabir: from *The Kabir Book* by Robert Bly, Copyright © 1971, 1977 by Robert Bly, © 1977 by the Seventies Press. Reprinted by permission of Beacon Press, Boston.

Howard Nemerov: from "Lines and Circularities," in *Gnomes and Occasions,* published by University of Chicago Press, 1973. Reprinted by permission of Margaret Nemerov.

Ursula Le Guin: "Artists," from *Always Coming Home,* © 1985 by Ursula K. Le Guin. Reprinted by permission of the author.

Alla Renée Bozarth: "What is Prayer?" from *Moving to the Edge of the World,* iUniverse.com, 2001. Reprinted by permission of the author.

Elizabeth Bishop: "Sonnet," from *Collected Poems,* 1927–1979, Farrar, Straus and Giroux. Reprinted by permission of Farrar, Straus and Giroux.

About Companion CDs

Maureen McCarthy Draper has produced two compact disc recordings to complement *The Nature of Music*. These two volumes contain many of the pieces described and high-lighted in the book, and offer an expanded and enhanced experience of *The Nature of Music*.

The Nature of Music
Volume One: Morning Music

The Nature of Music
Volume Two: Evening Music

These recordings are available at fine book and music stores everywhere or directly from:

Spring Hill Music
P.O. Box 800, Boulder, CO 80304
1-800-427-7680
www.springhillmedia.com